50 Vegan Cake and Pastries Recipes for Home

By: Kelly Johnson

Table of Contents

- Vegan Chocolate Cake
- Vegan Vanilla Cupcakes
- Vegan Lemon Cake
- Vegan Carrot Cake
- Vegan Red Velvet Cake
- Vegan Blueberry Muffins
- Vegan Banana Bread
- Vegan Pumpkin Pie
- Vegan Apple Crisp
- Vegan Coconut Macaroons
- Vegan Chocolate Chip Cookies
- Vegan Peanut Butter Brownies
- Vegan Raspberry Tart
- Vegan Strawberry Shortcake
- Vegan Cherry Pie
- Vegan Cinnamon Rolls
- Vegan Coffee Cake
- Vegan Oatmeal Cookies
- Vegan Almond Biscotti
- Vegan Gingerbread Cookies
- Vegan Key Lime Pie
- Vegan Peach Cobbler
- Vegan Pineapple Upside Down Cake
- Vegan Zucchini Bread
- Vegan Black Forest Cake
- Vegan Scones (Various flavors)
- Vegan Fig Newtons
- Vegan Pecan Pie Bars
- Vegan Cranberry Orange Bread
- Vegan Marble Cake
- Vegan Chocolate Truffles
- Vegan Almond Joy Bars
- Vegan Cheesecake (Various flavors)
- Vegan Pistachio Baklava
- Vegan Tiramisu

- Vegan Lemon Bars
- Vegan Date Squares
- Vegan Snickerdoodles
- Vegan Peanut Butter Cookies
- Vegan Chocolate Pudding Cake
- Vegan Mint Chocolate Chip Cupcakes
- Vegan Coconut Cream Pie
- Vegan Raspberry Swirl Cheesecake
- Vegan Orange Cranberry Scones
- Vegan Maple Pecan Pie
- Vegan Strawberry Rhubarb Crisp
- Vegan Blueberry Lemon Bundt Cake
- Vegan Chocolate Hazelnut Tart
- Vegan Mocha Brownies
- Vegan Cherry Chocolate Chip Muffins

Vegan Chocolate Cake

Ingredients:

For the Cake:

- 1 1/2 cups all-purpose flour
- 1 cup granulated sugar
- 1/3 cup unsweetened cocoa powder
- 1 teaspoon baking soda
- 1/2 teaspoon salt
- 1 cup brewed coffee (or water)
- 1/2 cup vegetable oil
- 2 tablespoons apple cider vinegar
- 2 teaspoons vanilla extract

For the Chocolate Frosting:

- 1/2 cup vegan butter, softened
- 2 cups powdered sugar
- 1/3 cup unsweetened cocoa powder
- 1 teaspoon vanilla extract
- 2-4 tablespoons non-dairy milk (as needed for consistency)

Instructions:

Preheat your oven to 350°F (175°C). Grease and flour an 8-inch round cake pan or line it with parchment paper.
In a large mixing bowl, sift together the flour, sugar, cocoa powder, baking soda, and salt.
In a separate bowl, mix together the brewed coffee (or water), vegetable oil, apple cider vinegar, and vanilla extract.
Pour the wet ingredients into the dry ingredients and mix until just combined. Be careful not to overmix.
Pour the batter into the prepared cake pan and spread it out evenly.
Bake in the preheated oven for 25-30 minutes, or until a toothpick inserted into the center comes out clean.

Remove the cake from the oven and let it cool in the pan for about 10 minutes before transferring it to a wire rack to cool completely.

While the cake is cooling, prepare the chocolate frosting. In a mixing bowl, beat the vegan butter until creamy.

Gradually add in the powdered sugar and cocoa powder, mixing until smooth and creamy.

Stir in the vanilla extract. If the frosting is too thick, add non-dairy milk, one tablespoon at a time, until you reach your desired consistency.

Once the cake has cooled completely, spread the frosting evenly over the top and sides of the cake.

Slice and serve the vegan chocolate cake, and enjoy!

This cake is rich, moist, and chocolaty, making it the perfect treat for any occasion!

Vegan Vanilla Cupcakes

Ingredients:

For the Cupcakes:

- 1 1/2 cups all-purpose flour
- 1 cup granulated sugar
- 1 teaspoon baking soda
- 1/2 teaspoon salt
- 1 cup non-dairy milk (such as almond milk or soy milk)
- 1/3 cup vegetable oil
- 2 tablespoons apple cider vinegar
- 2 teaspoons vanilla extract

For the Frosting:

- 1/2 cup vegan butter, softened
- 2 cups powdered sugar
- 1 teaspoon vanilla extract
- 1-2 tablespoons non-dairy milk (as needed for consistency)

Instructions:

Preheat your oven to 350°F (175°C). Line a muffin tin with paper liners.
In a large mixing bowl, whisk together the flour, sugar, baking soda, and salt.
In a separate bowl, mix together the non-dairy milk, vegetable oil, apple cider vinegar, and vanilla extract.
Pour the wet ingredients into the dry ingredients and mix until just combined. Be careful not to overmix.
Fill each muffin cup about two-thirds full with the cupcake batter.
Bake in the preheated oven for 18-20 minutes, or until a toothpick inserted into the center comes out clean.
Remove the cupcakes from the oven and let them cool in the muffin tin for a few minutes before transferring them to a wire rack to cool completely.
While the cupcakes are cooling, prepare the frosting. In a mixing bowl, beat the vegan butter until creamy.

Gradually add in the powdered sugar, mixing until smooth and creamy.
Stir in the vanilla extract. If the frosting is too thick, add non-dairy milk, one tablespoon at a time, until you reach your desired consistency.
Once the cupcakes have cooled completely, frost them with the vanilla frosting.
Optional: Decorate the cupcakes with sprinkles or other toppings of your choice.
Serve and enjoy these delicious vegan vanilla cupcakes!

These cupcakes are fluffy, moist, and bursting with vanilla flavor, making them a perfect treat for any occasion.

Vegan Lemon Cake

Ingredients:

For the Cake:

- 1 1/2 cups all-purpose flour
- 1 cup granulated sugar
- 1 teaspoon baking soda
- 1/2 teaspoon salt
- Zest of 2 lemons
- 1 cup non-dairy milk (such as almond milk or soy milk)
- 1/3 cup vegetable oil
- 2 tablespoons apple cider vinegar
- 2 tablespoons freshly squeezed lemon juice
- 1 teaspoon vanilla extract

For the Lemon Glaze:

- 1 cup powdered sugar
- 2-3 tablespoons freshly squeezed lemon juice

Instructions:

Preheat your oven to 350°F (175°C). Grease and flour an 8-inch round cake pan or line it with parchment paper.
In a large mixing bowl, whisk together the flour, sugar, baking soda, salt, and lemon zest.
In a separate bowl, mix together the non-dairy milk, vegetable oil, apple cider vinegar, lemon juice, and vanilla extract.
Pour the wet ingredients into the dry ingredients and mix until just combined. Be careful not to overmix.
Pour the batter into the prepared cake pan and spread it out evenly.
Bake in the preheated oven for 25-30 minutes, or until a toothpick inserted into the center comes out clean.
While the cake is baking, prepare the lemon glaze. In a small bowl, whisk together the powdered sugar and lemon juice until smooth.
Once the cake is done baking, remove it from the oven and let it cool in the pan for about 10 minutes before transferring it to a wire rack to cool completely.
Once the cake has cooled completely, drizzle the lemon glaze over the top.
Slice and serve the vegan lemon cake, and enjoy the bright, citrusy flavors!

This vegan lemon cake is moist, tangy, and bursting with lemon flavor. It's perfect for any occasion, from afternoon tea to dessert after dinner.

Vegan Carrot Cake

Ingredients:

For the Cake:

- 2 cups all-purpose flour
- 1 cup granulated sugar
- 1 teaspoon baking powder
- 1 teaspoon baking soda
- 1/2 teaspoon salt
- 2 teaspoons ground cinnamon
- 1/2 teaspoon ground nutmeg
- 1/2 cup unsweetened applesauce
- 1/2 cup vegetable oil
- 1/4 cup non-dairy milk (such as almond milk or soy milk)
- 1 teaspoon vanilla extract
- 2 cups grated carrots
- 1/2 cup crushed pineapple, drained
- 1/2 cup chopped walnuts or pecans (optional)
- 1/2 cup shredded coconut (optional)
- Vegan cream cheese frosting (see recipe below)

For the Vegan Cream Cheese Frosting:

- 1/2 cup vegan butter, softened
- 8 ounces vegan cream cheese, softened
- 4 cups powdered sugar
- 1 teaspoon vanilla extract

Instructions:

Preheat your oven to 350°F (175°C). Grease and flour a 9x13-inch baking pan or two 9-inch round cake pans.
In a large mixing bowl, whisk together the flour, sugar, baking powder, baking soda, salt, cinnamon, and nutmeg.

In a separate bowl, mix together the applesauce, vegetable oil, non-dairy milk, and vanilla extract.

Pour the wet ingredients into the dry ingredients and mix until just combined.

Fold in the grated carrots, crushed pineapple, chopped nuts (if using), and shredded coconut (if using) until evenly distributed.

Pour the batter into the prepared baking pan(s) and spread it out evenly.

Bake in the preheated oven for 30-35 minutes (for a 9x13-inch pan) or 25-30 minutes (for round pans), or until a toothpick inserted into the center comes out clean.

Remove the cake from the oven and let it cool completely in the pan(s) on a wire rack.

While the cake is cooling, prepare the vegan cream cheese frosting. In a mixing bowl, beat together the vegan butter and vegan cream cheese until smooth and creamy.

Gradually add in the powdered sugar, mixing until smooth and creamy.

Stir in the vanilla extract until well combined.

Once the cake has cooled completely, frost it with the vegan cream cheese frosting.

Slice and serve the vegan carrot cake, and enjoy the moist and flavorful treat!

This vegan carrot cake is wonderfully spiced, moist, and topped with a creamy vegan cream cheese frosting. It's perfect for any occasion, from birthdays to potlucks.

Vegan Red Velvet Cake

Ingredients:

For the Cake:

- 1 1/2 cups all-purpose flour
- 1 cup granulated sugar
- 1 teaspoon baking soda
- 1 tablespoon unsweetened cocoa powder
- 1/2 teaspoon salt
- 1 cup non-dairy milk (such as almond milk or soy milk)
- 1/2 cup vegetable oil
- 1 tablespoon apple cider vinegar
- 2 teaspoons vanilla extract
- 1-2 tablespoons red food coloring (vegan-friendly)
- Vegan cream cheese frosting (see recipe below)

For the Vegan Cream Cheese Frosting:

- 1/2 cup vegan butter, softened
- 8 ounces vegan cream cheese, softened
- 4 cups powdered sugar
- 1 teaspoon vanilla extract

Instructions:

Preheat your oven to 350°F (175°C). Grease and flour two 9-inch round cake pans.
In a large mixing bowl, whisk together the flour, sugar, baking soda, cocoa powder, and salt.
In a separate bowl, mix together the non-dairy milk, vegetable oil, apple cider vinegar, vanilla extract, and red food coloring until well combined.
Pour the wet ingredients into the dry ingredients and mix until just combined.
Divide the batter evenly between the prepared cake pans and spread it out evenly.
Bake in the preheated oven for 25-30 minutes, or until a toothpick inserted into the center comes out clean.

Remove the cakes from the oven and let them cool in the pans for 10 minutes before transferring them to a wire rack to cool completely.

While the cakes are cooling, prepare the vegan cream cheese frosting. In a mixing bowl, beat together the vegan butter and vegan cream cheese until smooth and creamy.

Gradually add in the powdered sugar, mixing until smooth and creamy.

Stir in the vanilla extract until well combined.

Once the cakes have cooled completely, frost the top of one cake layer with a generous amount of frosting. Place the second cake layer on top and frost the top and sides of the cake with the remaining frosting.

Slice and serve the vegan red velvet cake, and enjoy the rich, moist, and decadent treat!

This vegan red velvet cake is perfect for special occasions or anytime you're craving a classic dessert with a vegan twist.

Vegan Blueberry Muffins

Ingredients:

- 2 cups all-purpose flour
- 1/2 cup granulated sugar
- 2 teaspoons baking powder
- 1/2 teaspoon baking soda
- 1/4 teaspoon salt
- 1 cup non-dairy milk (such as almond milk or soy milk)
- 1/4 cup vegetable oil or melted coconut oil
- 1 tablespoon apple cider vinegar
- 1 teaspoon vanilla extract
- 1 1/2 cups fresh or frozen blueberries

Instructions:

Preheat your oven to 375°F (190°C). Line a muffin tin with paper liners or grease the cups lightly.
In a large mixing bowl, whisk together the flour, sugar, baking powder, baking soda, and salt.
In a separate bowl, mix together the non-dairy milk, vegetable oil, apple cider vinegar, and vanilla extract.
Pour the wet ingredients into the dry ingredients and stir until just combined. Be careful not to overmix; a few lumps are okay.
Gently fold in the blueberries until evenly distributed throughout the batter.
Divide the batter evenly among the prepared muffin cups, filling each about 3/4 full.
Optional: Sprinkle a little extra sugar on top of each muffin for a crunchy topping.
Bake in the preheated oven for 18-20 minutes, or until a toothpick inserted into the center of a muffin comes out clean.
Remove the muffins from the oven and let them cool in the muffin tin for a few minutes before transferring them to a wire rack to cool completely.
Serve and enjoy these delicious vegan blueberry muffins as a delightful breakfast or snack!

These muffins are moist, fluffy, and bursting with juicy blueberries. They're perfect for enjoying fresh out of the oven or storing for a quick grab-and-go snack throughout the week.

Vegan Banana Bread

Ingredients:

- 1 3/4 cups all-purpose flour
- 1 teaspoon baking powder
- 1/2 teaspoon baking soda
- 1/2 teaspoon salt
- 1 teaspoon ground cinnamon
- 3 large ripe bananas, mashed
- 1/2 cup brown sugar or coconut sugar
- 1/3 cup melted coconut oil or vegetable oil
- 1/4 cup non-dairy milk (such as almond milk or soy milk)
- 1 teaspoon vanilla extract
- 1/2 cup chopped walnuts or pecans (optional)

Instructions:

Preheat your oven to 350°F (175°C). Grease a 9x5-inch loaf pan or line it with parchment paper.

In a large mixing bowl, whisk together the flour, baking powder, baking soda, salt, and cinnamon.

In another bowl, mash the ripe bananas until smooth. Add the brown sugar, melted coconut oil (or vegetable oil), non-dairy milk, and vanilla extract. Stir until well combined.

Pour the wet ingredients into the dry ingredients and mix until just combined. Be careful not to overmix.

If using, fold in the chopped walnuts or pecans until evenly distributed throughout the batter.

Pour the batter into the prepared loaf pan and spread it out evenly.

Optional: Slice a banana in half lengthwise and place the halves on top of the batter for decoration.

Bake in the preheated oven for 50-60 minutes, or until a toothpick inserted into the center comes out clean.

If the top of the banana bread starts to brown too quickly, you can loosely cover it with aluminum foil during the last 15-20 minutes of baking.

Once baked, remove the banana bread from the oven and let it cool in the pan for about 10 minutes before transferring it to a wire rack to cool completely.

Slice and serve the vegan banana bread, and enjoy the moist and flavorful treat!

This vegan banana bread is perfect for breakfast, brunch, or as a delicious snack. It's moist, tender, and filled with the natural sweetness of ripe bananas.

Vegan Pumpkin Pie

Ingredients:

For the Crust:

- 1 1/4 cups all-purpose flour
- 1/4 teaspoon salt
- 1/3 cup vegan butter or coconut oil, cold and solid
- 3-4 tablespoons ice water

For the Filling:

- 1 (15-ounce) can pumpkin puree (not pumpkin pie filling)
- 1/2 cup full-fat coconut milk (from a can)
- 1/2 cup brown sugar or coconut sugar
- 1/4 cup maple syrup
- 2 tablespoons cornstarch or arrowroot powder
- 1 teaspoon vanilla extract
- 1 teaspoon ground cinnamon
- 1/2 teaspoon ground ginger
- 1/4 teaspoon ground nutmeg
- 1/4 teaspoon ground cloves
- 1/4 teaspoon salt

Instructions:

Preheat your oven to 375°F (190°C).
In a mixing bowl, combine the flour and salt. Cut in the cold vegan butter or coconut oil using a pastry cutter or fork until the mixture resembles coarse crumbs.
Gradually add the ice water, one tablespoon at a time, mixing until the dough comes together. Be careful not to overmix.
Shape the dough into a ball, then flatten it into a disk. Wrap it in plastic wrap and refrigerate for at least 30 minutes.

After chilling, roll out the dough on a lightly floured surface to fit a 9-inch pie dish. Carefully transfer the dough to the pie dish and trim any excess dough from the edges. Crimp the edges with a fork or your fingers.

In a large mixing bowl, whisk together all the filling ingredients until smooth and well combined.

Pour the filling into the prepared pie crust and smooth the top with a spatula.

Bake the pie in the preheated oven for 45-50 minutes, or until the filling is set and the crust is golden brown.

If the edges of the crust start to brown too quickly, you can cover them with aluminum foil halfway through baking.

Once baked, remove the pie from the oven and let it cool completely on a wire rack.

Refrigerate the cooled pie for at least 2 hours, or until chilled and set.

Serve slices of the vegan pumpkin pie with a dollop of whipped coconut cream or vegan vanilla ice cream, if desired.

Enjoy this delicious vegan pumpkin pie as a delightful dessert for your holiday gatherings or any time you're craving a taste of fall!

Vegan Apple Crisp

Ingredients:

For the Filling:

- 6 cups sliced apples (about 6 medium-sized apples)
- 1/4 cup maple syrup or agave nectar
- 1 tablespoon lemon juice
- 1 teaspoon vanilla extract
- 1 teaspoon ground cinnamon
- 1/4 teaspoon ground nutmeg
- 1 tablespoon cornstarch or arrowroot powder

For the Topping:

- 1 cup old-fashioned rolled oats (gluten-free if needed)
- 1/2 cup all-purpose flour (or almond flour for gluten-free)
- 1/2 cup packed brown sugar or coconut sugar
- 1/2 teaspoon ground cinnamon
- 1/4 teaspoon salt
- 1/2 cup vegan butter or coconut oil, melted

Instructions:

Preheat your oven to 350°F (175°C). Lightly grease an 8x8-inch baking dish or a similar-sized baking dish.

In a large mixing bowl, combine the sliced apples, maple syrup or agave nectar, lemon juice, vanilla extract, cinnamon, nutmeg, and cornstarch. Toss until the apples are evenly coated, then transfer the mixture to the prepared baking dish.

In another mixing bowl, combine the rolled oats, flour, brown sugar or coconut sugar, cinnamon, and salt. Stir until well combined.

Pour the melted vegan butter or coconut oil over the oat mixture and stir until the mixture is evenly moistened and crumbly.

Sprinkle the oat mixture evenly over the apples in the baking dish.

Bake in the preheated oven for 40-45 minutes, or until the topping is golden brown and the filling is bubbling.

Remove the apple crisp from the oven and let it cool for a few minutes before serving.

Serve the vegan apple crisp warm, optionally with a scoop of vegan vanilla ice cream or whipped coconut cream on top.

Enjoy this warm and comforting vegan apple crisp as a delightful dessert or a cozy treat on a chilly day!

Vegan Coconut Macaroons

Ingredients:

- 3 cups shredded coconut (unsweetened)
- 3/4 cup coconut cream (from a can of full-fat coconut milk)
- 1/2 cup maple syrup or agave nectar
- 1 teaspoon vanilla extract
- 1/4 teaspoon salt
- Optional: 1/2 cup vegan chocolate chips or melted chocolate for dipping (if desired)

Instructions:

Preheat your oven to 325°F (160°C). Line a baking sheet with parchment paper or a silicone baking mat.
In a mixing bowl, combine the shredded coconut, coconut cream, maple syrup or agave nectar, vanilla extract, and salt. Stir until well combined and the mixture holds together.
Using a small cookie scoop or tablespoon, scoop out portions of the coconut mixture and shape them into compact mounds using your hands. Place the mounds onto the prepared baking sheet, leaving some space between each one.
Bake in the preheated oven for 20-25 minutes, or until the edges of the macaroons are golden brown.
Remove the baking sheet from the oven and let the macaroons cool completely on the pan.
If desired, melt the chocolate chips in a microwave-safe bowl in 30-second intervals, stirring until smooth. Dip the bottoms of the cooled macaroons into the melted chocolate and place them back on the baking sheet to set.
Once the chocolate has set, serve and enjoy your delicious vegan coconut macaroons!

These vegan coconut macaroons are sweet, chewy, and packed with coconut flavor.

They make a delightful treat for any occasion and are perfect for sharing with friends and family.

Vegan Chocolate Chip Cookies

Ingredients:

- 1/2 cup vegan butter, softened
- 1/2 cup granulated sugar
- 1/4 cup brown sugar, packed
- 1 teaspoon vanilla extract
- 2 tablespoons non-dairy milk (such as almond milk or soy milk)
- 1 1/4 cups all-purpose flour
- 1/2 teaspoon baking soda
- 1/2 teaspoon salt
- 1 cup vegan chocolate chips

Instructions:

Preheat your oven to 350°F (175°C). Line a baking sheet with parchment paper or a silicone baking mat.
In a large mixing bowl, cream together the softened vegan butter, granulated sugar, and brown sugar until light and fluffy.
Add the vanilla extract and non-dairy milk to the creamed mixture and mix until well combined.
In a separate bowl, whisk together the all-purpose flour, baking soda, and salt.
Gradually add the dry ingredients to the wet ingredients, mixing until a dough forms.
Fold in the vegan chocolate chips until evenly distributed throughout the dough.
Using a cookie scoop or spoon, drop tablespoon-sized portions of dough onto the prepared baking sheet, spacing them about 2 inches apart.
Flatten each cookie slightly with the back of a spoon or your fingers.
Bake in the preheated oven for 10-12 minutes, or until the edges are golden brown.
Remove the baking sheet from the oven and let the cookies cool on the pan for a few minutes before transferring them to a wire rack to cool completely.
Once cooled, serve and enjoy your delicious vegan chocolate chip cookies!

These vegan chocolate chip cookies are soft, chewy, and loaded with chocolatey goodness. They're perfect for satisfying your sweet tooth and are sure to be a hit with vegans and non-vegans alike!

Vegan Peanut Butter Brownies

Ingredients:

For the Brownie Batter:

- 1/2 cup vegan butter, melted
- 3/4 cup granulated sugar
- 1/2 cup unsweetened applesauce
- 1 teaspoon vanilla extract
- 1/2 cup all-purpose flour
- 1/3 cup unsweetened cocoa powder
- 1/4 teaspoon baking powder
- 1/4 teaspoon salt
- 1/2 cup vegan chocolate chips

For the Peanut Butter Swirl:

- 1/2 cup creamy peanut butter
- 2 tablespoons maple syrup or agave nectar
- 2 tablespoons non-dairy milk (such as almond milk or soy milk)

Instructions:

Preheat your oven to 350°F (175°C). Grease or line an 8x8-inch baking pan with parchment paper.
In a large mixing bowl, whisk together the melted vegan butter, granulated sugar, applesauce, and vanilla extract until smooth.
In a separate bowl, sift together the all-purpose flour, cocoa powder, baking powder, and salt.
Gradually add the dry ingredients to the wet ingredients, stirring until just combined. Be careful not to overmix.
Fold in the vegan chocolate chips until evenly distributed throughout the batter.
In a small saucepan or microwave-safe bowl, melt the peanut butter, maple syrup or agave nectar, and non-dairy milk together until smooth and well combined.
Pour the brownie batter into the prepared baking pan and spread it out evenly.
Drizzle the peanut butter mixture over the brownie batter in diagonal lines.

Use a knife or toothpick to swirl the peanut butter mixture into the brownie batter, creating a marbled effect.

Bake in the preheated oven for 25-30 minutes, or until a toothpick inserted into the center comes out with a few moist crumbs.

Remove the pan from the oven and let the brownies cool completely in the pan on a wire rack.

Once cooled, slice into squares and serve. Enjoy your delicious vegan peanut butter brownies!

These vegan peanut butter brownies are rich, fudgy, and packed with peanut butter flavor. They're sure to be a hit with vegans and non-vegans alike!

Vegan Raspberry Tart

Ingredients:

For the Crust:

- 1 1/2 cups all-purpose flour
- 1/4 cup powdered sugar
- 1/4 teaspoon salt
- 1/2 cup vegan butter, chilled and cubed
- 3-4 tablespoons ice water

For the Filling:

- 2 cups fresh raspberries
- 1/4 cup granulated sugar
- 2 tablespoons cornstarch or arrowroot powder
- 1 tablespoon lemon juice
- 1 teaspoon vanilla extract

Instructions:

Preheat your oven to 375°F (190°C). Grease a 9-inch tart pan with a removable bottom or a pie dish.
In a food processor, combine the flour, powdered sugar, and salt. Add the chilled vegan butter and pulse until the mixture resembles coarse crumbs.
Gradually add the ice water, 1 tablespoon at a time, pulsing until the dough comes together and forms a ball.
Press the dough evenly into the bottom and up the sides of the prepared tart pan or pie dish.
Prick the bottom of the crust with a fork to prevent air bubbles from forming during baking.
Bake the crust in the preheated oven for 15-20 minutes, or until lightly golden brown. Remove from the oven and let it cool completely.
In a saucepan, combine the raspberries, granulated sugar, cornstarch or arrowroot powder, lemon juice, and vanilla extract.

Cook over medium heat, stirring constantly, until the mixture thickens and the raspberries break down slightly, about 5-7 minutes.
Remove the raspberry filling from the heat and let it cool slightly.
Pour the raspberry filling into the cooled tart crust, spreading it out evenly.
Refrigerate the tart for at least 2 hours, or until the filling is set.
Once set, slice and serve the vegan raspberry tart, optionally garnishing with fresh raspberries or a dusting of powdered sugar.

Enjoy this delicious and vibrant vegan raspberry tart as a delightful dessert for any occasion!

Vegan Strawberry Shortcake

Ingredients:

For the Shortcakes:

- 2 cups all-purpose flour
- 1/4 cup granulated sugar
- 1 tablespoon baking powder
- 1/2 teaspoon salt
- 1/2 cup vegan butter, cold and cubed
- 2/3 cup non-dairy milk (such as almond milk or soy milk)
- 1 teaspoon vanilla extract

For the Strawberries:

- 1 pound fresh strawberries, hulled and sliced
- 2-3 tablespoons granulated sugar (adjust to taste)
- Optional: 1 teaspoon lemon juice

For the Coconut Whipped Cream:

- 1 (14-ounce) can full-fat coconut milk, refrigerated overnight
- 2-3 tablespoons powdered sugar (adjust to taste)
- 1 teaspoon vanilla extract

Instructions:

Preheat your oven to 425°F (220°C). Line a baking sheet with parchment paper. In a large mixing bowl, whisk together the flour, sugar, baking powder, and salt. Add the cold cubed vegan butter to the dry ingredients. Using a pastry cutter or your fingers, cut the butter into the flour mixture until it resembles coarse crumbs.
In a small bowl, mix together the non-dairy milk and vanilla extract. Pour the wet ingredients into the flour mixture and stir until just combined. Be careful not to overmix.

Turn the dough out onto a lightly floured surface and gently knead it a few times until it comes together. Pat the dough into a circle about 3/4 inch thick.

Use a biscuit cutter or a drinking glass to cut out circles of dough. Place the dough circles onto the prepared baking sheet.

Bake in the preheated oven for 12-15 minutes, or until the shortcakes are golden brown on top.

While the shortcakes are baking, prepare the strawberries. In a mixing bowl, toss the sliced strawberries with the granulated sugar and lemon juice (if using). Let them sit for about 10 minutes to macerate.

To make the coconut whipped cream, remove the can of coconut milk from the refrigerator without shaking it. Open the can and scoop out the solid coconut cream that has risen to the top, leaving behind the liquid. Place the coconut cream in a mixing bowl.

Add powdered sugar and vanilla extract to the coconut cream. Using a hand mixer or stand mixer, beat the coconut cream until fluffy and smooth.

Once the shortcakes have cooled slightly, slice them in half horizontally. Place a spoonful of macerated strawberries on the bottom half of each shortcake, then top with a dollop of coconut whipped cream. Place the top half of the shortcake over the whipped cream.

Serve the vegan strawberry shortcakes immediately and enjoy!

These vegan strawberry shortcakes are a delightful summer dessert, perfect for showcasing fresh strawberries and topped with creamy coconut whipped cream. Enjoy this sweet treat with friends and family!

Vegan Cherry Pie

Ingredients:

For the Pie Crust:

- 2 1/2 cups all-purpose flour
- 1 tablespoon granulated sugar
- 1 teaspoon salt
- 1 cup vegan butter, cold and cubed
- 6-8 tablespoons ice water

For the Cherry Filling:

- 4 cups fresh or frozen cherries, pitted
- 1/2 cup granulated sugar
- 2 tablespoons cornstarch or arrowroot powder
- 1 tablespoon lemon juice
- 1/2 teaspoon almond extract (optional)
- 1/4 teaspoon salt

Instructions:

Preheat your oven to 375°F (190°C). Grease a 9-inch pie dish.
In a large mixing bowl, whisk together the flour, sugar, and salt.
Add the cold cubed vegan butter to the flour mixture. Using a pastry cutter or your fingers, cut the butter into the flour mixture until it resembles coarse crumbs.
Gradually add the ice water, 1 tablespoon at a time, mixing with a fork until the dough starts to come together.
Turn the dough out onto a lightly floured surface and gently knead it a few times until it forms a ball. Divide the dough in half, shape each half into a disk, wrap them in plastic wrap, and refrigerate for at least 30 minutes.
While the dough is chilling, prepare the cherry filling. In a saucepan, combine the cherries, sugar, cornstarch or arrowroot powder, lemon juice, almond extract (if using), and salt. Cook over medium heat, stirring frequently, until the mixture

thickens and the cherries release their juices, about 5-7 minutes. Remove from heat and let it cool slightly.

Roll out one disk of dough on a lightly floured surface into a circle about 12 inches in diameter. Carefully transfer the rolled-out dough to the prepared pie dish.

Pour the cherry filling into the pie crust, spreading it out evenly.

Roll out the second disk of dough into a circle about 12 inches in diameter. Carefully place it over the cherry filling.

Trim any excess dough from the edges and crimp the edges of the pie crust to seal.

Optional: Cut slits in the top crust to allow steam to escape during baking, or create a lattice crust.

Bake the pie in the preheated oven for 45-50 minutes, or until the crust is golden brown and the filling is bubbling.

Remove the pie from the oven and let it cool completely on a wire rack before slicing and serving.

Serve slices of the vegan cherry pie with a dollop of vegan whipped cream or dairy-free ice cream, if desired.

Enjoy this delicious vegan cherry pie as a delightful dessert for any occasion!

Vegan Cinnamon Rolls

Ingredients:

For the Dough:

- 1 cup unsweetened non-dairy milk (such as almond milk or soy milk)
- 1/4 cup vegan butter, melted
- 1/4 cup granulated sugar
- 1 packet (2 1/4 teaspoons) active dry yeast
- 3 1/2 cups all-purpose flour, plus more for dusting
- 1/2 teaspoon salt

For the Filling:

- 1/3 cup vegan butter, softened
- 3/4 cup brown sugar, packed
- 2 tablespoons ground cinnamon

For the Vegan Cream Cheese Glaze:

- 4 ounces vegan cream cheese, softened
- 1/4 cup vegan butter, softened
- 1 cup powdered sugar
- 1 teaspoon vanilla extract

Instructions:

In a small saucepan, heat the non-dairy milk until warm but not boiling. Remove from heat and stir in the melted vegan butter and granulated sugar. Let it cool until it reaches about 110°F (43°C).

Sprinkle the yeast over the warm milk mixture and let it sit for 5-10 minutes, until it becomes frothy.

In a large mixing bowl, combine the flour and salt. Pour the yeast mixture over the flour mixture and stir until a dough forms.

Knead the dough on a lightly floured surface for 5-7 minutes, until smooth and elastic.

Place the dough in a greased bowl, cover with a clean kitchen towel or plastic wrap, and let it rise in a warm place for about 1 hour, or until doubled in size.

Once the dough has risen, punch it down and roll it out on a lightly floured surface into a rectangle, about 12x18 inches.

Spread the softened vegan butter evenly over the rolled-out dough, leaving a small border around the edges.

In a small bowl, mix together the brown sugar and ground cinnamon. Sprinkle the cinnamon sugar mixture evenly over the buttered dough.

Starting from one long edge, tightly roll the dough into a log. Use a sharp knife to slice the log into 12 equal-sized rolls.

Place the rolls in a greased 9x13-inch baking dish, leaving a little space between each roll.

Cover the baking dish with a clean kitchen towel or plastic wrap and let the rolls rise in a warm place for another 30-45 minutes, until they have doubled in size.

Preheat your oven to 350°F (175°C). Once the rolls have risen, bake them in the preheated oven for 25-30 minutes, until golden brown.

While the rolls are baking, prepare the vegan cream cheese glaze. In a mixing bowl, beat together the softened vegan cream cheese and vegan butter until smooth. Gradually add the powdered sugar and vanilla extract, mixing until creamy.

Once the rolls are done baking, remove them from the oven and let them cool slightly. Drizzle the vegan cream cheese glaze over the warm rolls.

Serve the vegan cinnamon rolls warm and enjoy!

These vegan cinnamon rolls are soft, fluffy, and filled with sweet cinnamon goodness.

They're perfect for breakfast, brunch, or a tasty treat any time of day!

Vegan Coffee Cake

Ingredients:

For the Streusel Topping:

- 1/2 cup all-purpose flour
- 1/2 cup brown sugar, packed
- 1 teaspoon ground cinnamon
- 1/4 cup vegan butter, melted

For the Cake Batter:

- 2 cups all-purpose flour
- 1 teaspoon baking powder
- 1/2 teaspoon baking soda
- 1/4 teaspoon salt
- 1/2 cup vegan butter, softened
- 3/4 cup granulated sugar
- 1 cup unsweetened applesauce
- 1/4 cup non-dairy milk (such as almond milk or soy milk)
- 1 teaspoon vanilla extract

Instructions:

Preheat your oven to 350°F (175°C). Grease a 9x9-inch square baking pan.
In a small mixing bowl, prepare the streusel topping by combining the flour, brown sugar, and cinnamon. Stir in the melted vegan butter until crumbly. Set aside.
In a medium mixing bowl, whisk together the flour, baking powder, baking soda, and salt for the cake batter.
In a large mixing bowl, cream together the softened vegan butter and granulated sugar until light and fluffy.
Stir in the applesauce, non-dairy milk, and vanilla extract until well combined.
Gradually add the dry ingredients to the wet ingredients, mixing until just combined. Be careful not to overmix.
Pour half of the cake batter into the prepared baking pan and spread it out evenly.
Sprinkle half of the streusel topping over the batter in the pan.
Pour the remaining cake batter over the streusel layer and spread it out evenly.

Sprinkle the remaining streusel topping over the top of the cake batter.

Bake in the preheated oven for 35-40 minutes, or until a toothpick inserted into the center comes out clean.

Remove the coffee cake from the oven and let it cool in the pan for about 10 minutes before slicing and serving.

Serve the vegan coffee cake warm or at room temperature, and enjoy!

This vegan coffee cake is perfect for breakfast, brunch, or as a sweet treat with your afternoon coffee or tea. It's moist, tender, and filled with delicious cinnamon streusel flavor!

Vegan Oatmeal Cookies

Ingredients:

- 1 cup rolled oats (old-fashioned oats)
- 3/4 cup all-purpose flour
- 1/2 teaspoon baking soda
- 1/2 teaspoon ground cinnamon
- 1/4 teaspoon salt
- 1/2 cup vegan butter, softened
- 1/2 cup brown sugar, packed
- 1/4 cup granulated sugar
- 1 flax egg (1 tablespoon ground flaxseed + 3 tablespoons water)
- 1 teaspoon vanilla extract
- 1/2 cup raisins or vegan chocolate chips (optional)

Instructions:

Preheat your oven to 350°F (175°C). Line a baking sheet with parchment paper or a silicone baking mat.
In a medium mixing bowl, whisk together the rolled oats, all-purpose flour, baking soda, ground cinnamon, and salt.
In a large mixing bowl, cream together the softened vegan butter, brown sugar, and granulated sugar until light and fluffy.
Prepare the flax egg by mixing together 1 tablespoon of ground flaxseed with 3 tablespoons of water in a small bowl. Let it sit for a few minutes to thicken.
Add the flax egg and vanilla extract to the creamed butter and sugar mixture. Mix until well combined.
Gradually add the dry ingredients to the wet ingredients, mixing until just combined. Be careful not to overmix.
Fold in the raisins or vegan chocolate chips, if using.
Drop tablespoon-sized portions of dough onto the prepared baking sheet, spacing them about 2 inches apart.
Use your fingers or the back of a spoon to gently flatten each cookie dough portion.
Bake in the preheated oven for 10-12 minutes, or until the edges are golden brown.
Remove the cookies from the oven and let them cool on the baking sheet for a few minutes before transferring them to a wire rack to cool completely.

Once cooled, serve and enjoy your delicious vegan oatmeal cookies!

These vegan oatmeal cookies are chewy, flavorful, and perfect for enjoying as a sweet snack or dessert. They're easy to make and sure to be a hit with vegans and non-vegans alike!

Vegan Almond Biscotti

Ingredients:

- 2 cups all-purpose flour
- 3/4 cup granulated sugar
- 1 teaspoon baking powder
- 1/4 teaspoon salt
- 1/2 cup unsweetened almond milk (or any other non-dairy milk)
- 1/4 cup melted coconut oil (or any other vegetable oil)
- 1 teaspoon vanilla extract
- 1/2 teaspoon almond extract
- 1/2 cup sliced almonds

Instructions:

Preheat your oven to 350°F (175°C). Line a baking sheet with parchment paper.
In a large mixing bowl, whisk together the flour, sugar, baking powder, and salt.
In a separate bowl, mix together the almond milk, melted coconut oil, vanilla extract, and almond extract.
Pour the wet ingredients into the dry ingredients and mix until a dough forms.
Fold in the sliced almonds until evenly distributed throughout the dough.
Transfer the dough onto a lightly floured surface and shape it into a long log, about 12 inches long and 3-4 inches wide.
Place the log onto the prepared baking sheet and flatten it slightly with your hands.
Bake in the preheated oven for 25-30 minutes, or until the biscotti log is firm and lightly golden brown.
Remove the biscotti log from the oven and let it cool on the baking sheet for about 10 minutes.
Using a sharp knife, slice the biscotti log diagonally into 1/2-inch thick slices.
Place the biscotti slices back onto the baking sheet, cut side down.
Return the biscotti slices to the oven and bake for an additional 10-15 minutes, or until they are golden brown and crispy.
Remove the biscotti from the oven and let them cool completely on a wire rack.
Once cooled, serve and enjoy your delicious vegan almond biscotti with a cup of coffee or tea!

These vegan almond biscotti are crunchy, flavorful, and perfect for dipping into your favorite hot beverage. They make a delightful treat for any time of day!

Vegan Gingerbread Cookies

Ingredients:

- 2 1/2 cups all-purpose flour
- 1/2 teaspoon baking soda
- 1/2 teaspoon baking powder
- 1/2 teaspoon salt
- 1 tablespoon ground ginger
- 1 teaspoon ground cinnamon
- 1/4 teaspoon ground cloves
- 1/4 teaspoon ground nutmeg
- 1/2 cup vegan butter, softened
- 1/2 cup brown sugar, packed
- 1/2 cup molasses
- 1 tablespoon flaxseed meal + 3 tablespoons water (to make flaxseed egg)
- 1 teaspoon vanilla extract

Instructions:

In a small bowl, prepare the flaxseed egg by mixing together 1 tablespoon of flaxseed meal with 3 tablespoons of water. Let it sit for 5-10 minutes to thicken.
In a large mixing bowl, whisk together the flour, baking soda, baking powder, salt, ginger, cinnamon, cloves, and nutmeg until well combined.
In another large mixing bowl, cream together the softened vegan butter and brown sugar until light and fluffy.
Add the molasses, flaxseed egg, and vanilla extract to the creamed butter and sugar mixture. Mix until well combined.
Gradually add the dry ingredients to the wet ingredients, mixing until a dough forms. If the dough is too sticky, you can add a little more flour until it reaches a workable consistency.
Divide the dough into two equal portions, flatten them into disks, wrap them in plastic wrap, and refrigerate for at least 1 hour (or up to overnight).
Preheat your oven to 350°F (175°C). Line a baking sheet with parchment paper.
Remove one portion of the dough from the refrigerator and let it sit at room temperature for a few minutes to soften slightly.
Roll out the dough on a lightly floured surface to about 1/4 inch thick.
Use cookie cutters to cut out shapes from the dough and place them onto the prepared baking sheet, leaving a little space between each cookie.

Gather up any scraps of dough, reroll them, and cut out more cookies until all the dough is used.

Bake the cookies in the preheated oven for 8-10 minutes, or until the edges are set and the tops are slightly firm to the touch.

Remove the cookies from the oven and let them cool on the baking sheet for a few minutes before transferring them to a wire rack to cool completely.

Once cooled, decorate the cookies with vegan icing or enjoy them as is.

These vegan gingerbread cookies are perfect for the holiday season or anytime you're craving a festive treat. They're wonderfully spiced, soft, and full of flavor!

Vegan Key Lime Pie

Ingredients:

For the Crust:

- 1 1/2 cups vegan graham cracker crumbs (or crushed vegan graham crackers)
- 1/4 cup granulated sugar
- 1/3 cup melted coconut oil (or vegan butter)

For the Filling:

- 1 (14-ounce) can full-fat coconut milk, chilled in the refrigerator overnight
- 1/2 cup key lime juice (freshly squeezed if possible)
- 1 tablespoon key lime zest (from about 4-5 key limes)
- 1/2 cup maple syrup or agave nectar
- 1 teaspoon vanilla extract
- Pinch of salt

Instructions:

Preheat your oven to 350°F (175°C). Grease a 9-inch pie dish.
In a mixing bowl, combine the vegan graham cracker crumbs, granulated sugar, and melted coconut oil. Stir until the mixture resembles wet sand.
Press the mixture into the bottom and up the sides of the prepared pie dish to form the crust.
Bake the crust in the preheated oven for 10-12 minutes, or until lightly golden brown. Remove from the oven and let it cool completely.
While the crust is cooling, prepare the filling. Open the chilled can of coconut milk and scoop out the solid coconut cream that has risen to the top, leaving behind the liquid. Place the coconut cream in a mixing bowl.
Add the key lime juice, key lime zest, maple syrup or agave nectar, vanilla extract, and a pinch of salt to the coconut cream. Beat with a hand mixer or stand mixer until smooth and creamy.
Pour the filling into the cooled pie crust and smooth the top with a spatula.
Refrigerate the pie for at least 4 hours, or until set.
Once set, slice and serve the vegan key lime pie.

Optionally, garnish with additional key lime zest or slices before serving.

Enjoy this refreshing and tangy vegan key lime pie as a delightful dessert for any occasion!

Vegan Peach Cobbler

Ingredients:

For the Peach Filling:

- 6 cups fresh or frozen peach slices (about 6-8 peaches)
- 1/2 cup granulated sugar
- 2 tablespoons cornstarch or arrowroot powder
- 1 tablespoon lemon juice
- 1 teaspoon vanilla extract
- 1/2 teaspoon ground cinnamon
- 1/4 teaspoon ground nutmeg

For the Cobbler Topping:

- 1 1/2 cups all-purpose flour
- 1/2 cup granulated sugar
- 2 teaspoons baking powder
- 1/2 teaspoon salt
- 1/2 cup vegan butter, melted
- 1/2 cup unsweetened almond milk (or any other non-dairy milk)
- 1 teaspoon vanilla extract

Instructions:

Preheat your oven to 375°F (190°C). Grease a 9x13-inch baking dish.
In a large mixing bowl, combine the peach slices, granulated sugar, cornstarch or arrowroot powder, lemon juice, vanilla extract, ground cinnamon, and ground nutmeg. Toss until the peaches are evenly coated, then transfer the mixture to the prepared baking dish.
In another mixing bowl, whisk together the all-purpose flour, granulated sugar, baking powder, and salt for the cobbler topping.
Add the melted vegan butter, unsweetened almond milk, and vanilla extract to the dry ingredients. Stir until just combined, being careful not to overmix.
Drop spoonfuls of the cobbler topping over the peach filling in the baking dish, spreading it out evenly.

Bake in the preheated oven for 35-40 minutes, or until the cobbler topping is golden brown and the peach filling is bubbly.
Remove the cobbler from the oven and let it cool slightly before serving.
Serve the vegan peach cobbler warm, optionally topped with vegan vanilla ice cream or whipped coconut cream.

Enjoy this deliciously comforting vegan peach cobbler as a delightful dessert, perfect for sharing with friends and family!

Vegan Pineapple Upside Down Cake

Ingredients:

For the Pineapple Topping:

- 1/4 cup vegan butter
- 2/3 cup brown sugar, packed
- 1 can (20 oz) pineapple slices in juice, drained (reserve the juice)
- Maraschino cherries (optional)

For the Cake Batter:

- 1 1/2 cups all-purpose flour
- 1 cup granulated sugar
- 1 teaspoon baking soda
- 1/2 teaspoon salt
- 1/3 cup vegetable oil
- 1 cup pineapple juice (reserved from the canned pineapple)
- 1 tablespoon apple cider vinegar
- 1 teaspoon vanilla extract

Instructions:

Preheat your oven to 350°F (175°C). Grease a 9-inch round cake pan.
In a small saucepan, melt the vegan butter over medium heat. Add the brown sugar and stir until melted and bubbly. Pour the mixture into the prepared cake pan and spread it out evenly.
Arrange the pineapple slices on top of the brown sugar mixture in the cake pan. You can place a maraschino cherry in the center of each pineapple slice if desired.
In a large mixing bowl, whisk together the flour, granulated sugar, baking soda, and salt.
In a separate bowl, whisk together the vegetable oil, pineapple juice, apple cider vinegar, and vanilla extract.
Pour the wet ingredients into the dry ingredients and mix until just combined. Be careful not to overmix.

Pour the cake batter over the pineapple slices in the cake pan, spreading it out evenly.

Bake in the preheated oven for 35-40 minutes, or until a toothpick inserted into the center of the cake comes out clean.

Remove the cake from the oven and let it cool in the pan for about 10 minutes.

Place a serving plate upside-down over the top of the cake pan. Carefully invert the cake onto the plate. Lift off the cake pan, revealing the pineapple topping.

Let the cake cool completely before slicing and serving.

Serve slices of the vegan pineapple upside-down cake on their own or with a dollop of vegan whipped cream or dairy-free ice cream, if desired.

Enjoy this delicious vegan pineapple upside-down cake as a delightful dessert, perfect for any occasion!

Vegan Zucchini Bread

Ingredients:

- 2 cups shredded zucchini (about 2 medium zucchinis)
- 1/2 cup unsweetened applesauce
- 1/2 cup melted coconut oil or vegetable oil
- 1 cup granulated sugar
- 1 teaspoon vanilla extract
- 2 cups all-purpose flour
- 1 teaspoon baking powder
- 1/2 teaspoon baking soda
- 1/2 teaspoon salt
- 1 teaspoon ground cinnamon
- 1/2 teaspoon ground nutmeg
- Optional: 1/2 cup chopped nuts or vegan chocolate chips

Instructions:

Preheat your oven to 350°F (175°C). Grease a 9x5-inch loaf pan or line it with parchment paper.
In a large mixing bowl, combine the shredded zucchini, unsweetened applesauce, melted coconut oil or vegetable oil, granulated sugar, and vanilla extract. Stir until well combined.
In a separate bowl, whisk together the all-purpose flour, baking powder, baking soda, salt, ground cinnamon, and ground nutmeg.
Gradually add the dry ingredients to the wet ingredients, stirring until just combined. Be careful not to overmix.
If desired, fold in the chopped nuts or vegan chocolate chips until evenly distributed throughout the batter.
Pour the batter into the prepared loaf pan and spread it out evenly.
Bake in the preheated oven for 50-60 minutes, or until a toothpick inserted into the center comes out clean.
Remove the zucchini bread from the oven and let it cool in the pan for about 10 minutes.
Once cooled slightly, transfer the zucchini bread to a wire rack to cool completely before slicing and serving.
Serve slices of the vegan zucchini bread as a delicious snack or breakfast treat.

Enjoy this moist and flavorful vegan zucchini bread, perfect for using up an abundance of fresh zucchini from the garden!

Vegan Black Forest Cake

Ingredients:

For the Cake:

- 1 1/2 cups all-purpose flour
- 1 cup granulated sugar
- 1/4 cup cocoa powder
- 1 teaspoon baking soda
- 1/2 teaspoon salt
- 1 cup almond milk (or any non-dairy milk)
- 1/3 cup vegetable oil
- 1 tablespoon apple cider vinegar
- 1 teaspoon vanilla extract

For the Filling:

- 1 (14-ounce) can cherry pie filling (make sure it's vegan)
- 2 cups vegan whipped cream or coconut whipped cream

For Decoration:

- Vegan chocolate shavings
- Maraschino cherries (optional)

Instructions:

1. Preheat your oven to 350°F (175°C). Grease and flour two 9-inch round cake pans.

2. Make the Cake:

- In a large mixing bowl, whisk together the flour, sugar, cocoa powder, baking soda, and salt until well combined.
- In a separate bowl, mix together the almond milk, vegetable oil, apple cider vinegar, and vanilla extract.
- Pour the wet ingredients into the dry ingredients and mix until just combined. Do not overmix.
- Divide the batter evenly between the prepared cake pans.

- Bake in the preheated oven for 25-30 minutes, or until a toothpick inserted into the center of the cakes comes out clean.
- Remove the cakes from the oven and let them cool in the pans for 10 minutes. Then, transfer them to a wire rack to cool completely.

3. Assemble the Cake:

- Once the cakes are completely cooled, place one cake layer on a serving plate.
- Spread a layer of cherry pie filling evenly over the cake layer.
- Top with a layer of whipped cream.
- Place the second cake layer on top and press down gently.
- Frost the top and sides of the cake with the remaining whipped cream.
- Decorate the top of the cake with vegan chocolate shavings and maraschino cherries, if desired.

4. Serve and Enjoy!

- Slice the cake and serve. Enjoy your delicious Vegan Black Forest Cake!

This cake is sure to be a hit with vegans and non-vegans alike!

Vegan Scones (Various flavors)

Ingredients:

- 2 cups all-purpose flour
- 1/4 cup granulated sugar
- 1 tablespoon baking powder
- 1/2 teaspoon salt
- 1/3 cup vegan butter or coconut oil, chilled
- 1/2 cup non-dairy milk (such as almond milk, soy milk, or oat milk)
- 1 teaspoon vanilla extract

For Flavor Variations:

Choose one of the following options or mix and match to create different flavored scones:

For Blueberry Scones:

- 1/2 cup fresh or frozen blueberries

For Chocolate Chip Scones:

- 1/2 cup vegan chocolate chips

For Lemon Poppy Seed Scones:

- Zest of 1 lemon
- 1 tablespoon poppy seeds

For Cranberry Orange Scones:

- 1/2 cup dried cranberries
- Zest of 1 orange

For Cinnamon Raisin Scones:

- 1/2 cup raisins
- 1 teaspoon ground cinnamon

Instructions:

1. Preheat your oven to 400°F (200°C). Line a baking sheet with parchment paper.

2. Make the Dough:

    - In a large mixing bowl, whisk together the flour, sugar, baking powder, and salt.
    - Add the chilled vegan butter or coconut oil to the dry ingredients. Using a pastry cutter or your fingers, work the butter or oil into the flour mixture until it resembles coarse crumbs.
    - Stir in your desired flavorings (blueberries, chocolate chips, lemon zest, poppy seeds, cranberries, orange zest, raisins, cinnamon, etc.).

3. Form the Dough:

    - Make a well in the center of the mixture and pour in the non-dairy milk and vanilla extract.
    - Gently stir until the dough comes together. Be careful not to overmix.
    - Turn the dough out onto a lightly floured surface and gently knead it a few times until it holds together.

4. Shape and Cut the Scones:

    - Flatten the dough into a circle about 1-inch thick.
    - Using a sharp knife or a biscuit cutter, cut the dough into wedges or rounds, depending on your preference.
    - Place the scones on the prepared baking sheet, leaving some space between each one.

5. Bake the Scones:

    - Bake in the preheated oven for 12-15 minutes, or until the scones are lightly golden brown on top.

- Remove from the oven and let cool on the baking sheet for a few minutes before transferring to a wire rack to cool completely.

6. Serve and Enjoy!

- Serve the scones warm or at room temperature with your favorite vegan butter, jam, or cream.
- Enjoy your delicious homemade Vegan Scones with your chosen flavor variation!

Feel free to experiment with other flavor combinations by adding nuts, seeds, spices, or dried fruits to the basic scone dough.

Vegan Fig Newtons

Ingredients:

For the Dough:

- 1 1/2 cups all-purpose flour
- 1/2 teaspoon baking powder
- 1/4 teaspoon salt
- 1/4 cup vegan butter, softened
- 1/4 cup granulated sugar
- 1/4 cup maple syrup
- 1 teaspoon vanilla extract

For the Fig Filling:

- 1 1/2 cups dried figs, stems removed and chopped
- 1/2 cup water
- 1 tablespoon lemon juice
- Zest of 1 lemon
- 1/4 teaspoon ground cinnamon

Instructions:

1. Make the Fig Filling:

- In a saucepan, combine the chopped dried figs, water, lemon juice, lemon zest, and ground cinnamon.
- Bring the mixture to a simmer over medium heat.
- Reduce the heat to low and cook for about 10-15 minutes, stirring occasionally, until the figs are soft and the mixture has thickened.
- Remove from heat and let the filling cool slightly.

2. Make the Dough:

- In a mixing bowl, whisk together the flour, baking powder, and salt.
- In another bowl, cream together the softened vegan butter, granulated sugar, maple syrup, and vanilla extract until smooth and creamy.

- Gradually add the dry ingredients to the wet ingredients, mixing until a dough forms.
- Divide the dough into two equal portions, shape them into discs, wrap them in plastic wrap, and refrigerate for at least 30 minutes to firm up.

3. Assemble the Fig Newtons:

- Preheat your oven to 350°F (175°C). Line a baking sheet with parchment paper.
- Place one portion of the chilled dough between two sheets of parchment paper and roll it out into a rectangle about 1/4 inch thick.
- Spread half of the fig filling evenly over the dough, leaving a small border around the edges.
- Carefully roll the dough into a log, using the parchment paper to help lift and roll.
- Repeat the process with the remaining dough and fig filling.
- Place the logs seam side down on the prepared baking sheet.
- Using a sharp knife, score the tops of the logs at 1-inch intervals.

4. Bake the Fig Newtons:

- Bake in the preheated oven for 20-25 minutes, or until the dough is lightly golden brown.
- Remove from the oven and let cool on the baking sheet for a few minutes before transferring to a wire rack to cool completely.

5. Slice and Serve:

- Once the Fig Newtons are completely cool, use a sharp knife to slice them into individual cookies along the scored lines.
- Serve and enjoy your homemade Vegan Fig Newtons!

These Vegan Fig Newtons are a delightful treat that's perfect for snacking or enjoying with a cup of tea. Store any leftovers in an airtight container at room temperature for up to several days.

Vegan Pecan Pie Bars

Ingredients:

For the Crust:

- 1 1/2 cups all-purpose flour
- 1/2 cup vegan butter, softened
- 1/4 cup granulated sugar
- 1/4 teaspoon salt

For the Pecan Filling:

- 1 cup maple syrup
- 1/2 cup coconut sugar or brown sugar
- 1/4 cup melted coconut oil
- 1 tablespoon ground flaxseed meal mixed with 3 tablespoons water (to replace eggs)
- 1 tablespoon cornstarch
- 1 teaspoon vanilla extract
- 2 cups pecan halves

Instructions:

**1. Preheat your oven to 350°F (175°C). Line an 8x8 inch baking dish with parchment paper, leaving some overhang on the sides for easy removal.

2. Make the Crust:

- In a mixing bowl, combine the softened vegan butter, granulated sugar, and salt. Mix until creamy.
- Gradually add the flour and mix until a dough forms.
- Press the dough evenly into the bottom of the prepared baking dish.
- Bake the crust in the preheated oven for 15-18 minutes, or until lightly golden brown. Remove from the oven and set aside.

3. Make the Pecan Filling:

- In a separate mixing bowl, whisk together the maple syrup, coconut sugar, melted coconut oil, flaxseed mixture, cornstarch, and vanilla extract until well combined.
- Stir in the pecan halves until they are evenly coated with the mixture.

4. Assemble and Bake:

- Pour the pecan filling over the baked crust, spreading it out evenly.
- Return the baking dish to the oven and bake for an additional 25-30 minutes, or until the filling is set and golden brown on top.
- Remove from the oven and let the pecan pie bars cool completely in the baking dish.

5. Slice and Serve:

- Once cooled, use the parchment paper overhang to lift the pecan pie bars out of the baking dish.
- Transfer to a cutting board and slice into bars or squares.
- Serve and enjoy your delicious Vegan Pecan Pie Bars!

These bars are perfect for any occasion, from holiday gatherings to afternoon snacks.

Store any leftovers in an airtight container at room temperature for up to several days.

Enjoy!

Vegan Cranberry Orange Bread

Ingredients:

- 2 cups all-purpose flour
- 3/4 cup granulated sugar
- 1 tablespoon baking powder
- 1/2 teaspoon baking soda
- 1/2 teaspoon salt
- Zest of 1 orange
- 3/4 cup freshly squeezed orange juice (from about 2 oranges)
- 1/3 cup melted coconut oil or vegetable oil
- 1 teaspoon vanilla extract
- 1 cup fresh cranberries, chopped
- Optional: 1/2 cup chopped nuts (such as walnuts or pecans)

Instructions:

**1. Preheat your oven to 350°F (175°C). Grease and flour a 9x5-inch loaf pan or line it with parchment paper.

2. Prepare the Batter:

- In a large mixing bowl, whisk together the flour, sugar, baking powder, baking soda, salt, and orange zest until well combined.
- In a separate bowl, mix together the freshly squeezed orange juice, melted coconut oil or vegetable oil, and vanilla extract.
- Pour the wet ingredients into the dry ingredients and stir until just combined. Be careful not to overmix.
- Gently fold in the chopped cranberries and nuts, if using.

3. Bake the Bread:

- Pour the batter into the prepared loaf pan, spreading it out evenly.
- Bake in the preheated oven for 50-60 minutes, or until a toothpick inserted into the center of the bread comes out clean.
- If the top of the bread starts to brown too quickly, you can loosely cover it with aluminum foil halfway through baking.
- Once baked, remove the bread from the oven and let it cool in the pan for 10 minutes.

- Then, transfer the bread to a wire rack to cool completely.

4. Serve and Enjoy:

    - Once the bread has cooled completely, slice it into thick slices.
    - Serve and enjoy your delicious Vegan Cranberry Orange Bread!
    - You can store any leftovers in an airtight container at room temperature for up to several days, or freeze slices for longer storage.

This bread is perfect for breakfast, brunch, or as a tasty snack any time of day. The combination of tangy cranberries and citrusy orange flavors is sure to be a hit!

Vegan Marble Cake

Ingredients:

For the Vanilla Batter:

- 1 3/4 cups all-purpose flour
- 1 cup granulated sugar
- 1 teaspoon baking powder
- 1/2 teaspoon baking soda
- 1/2 teaspoon salt
- 1 cup almond milk (or any non-dairy milk)
- 1/2 cup vegetable oil
- 2 teaspoons vanilla extract

For the Chocolate Batter:

- 1/4 cup cocoa powder
- 1/4 cup hot water

Instructions:

**1. Preheat your oven to 350°F (175°C). Grease and flour a 9x5-inch loaf pan or line it with parchment paper for easy removal.

2. Make the Vanilla Batter:

- In a large mixing bowl, whisk together the flour, sugar, baking powder, baking soda, and salt until well combined.
- Add the almond milk, vegetable oil, and vanilla extract to the dry ingredients. Mix until smooth and well combined.

3. Make the Chocolate Batter:

- In a small bowl, mix together the cocoa powder and hot water until smooth to create a chocolate paste.

4. Assemble the Marble Cake:

- Pour half of the vanilla batter into the prepared loaf pan, spreading it out evenly.
- Add dollops of the chocolate paste on top of the vanilla batter.
- Use a butter knife or skewer to swirl the chocolate paste into the vanilla batter, creating a marble effect.
- Pour the remaining vanilla batter over the chocolate swirls, spreading it out evenly.

5. Bake the Cake:

- Place the loaf pan in the preheated oven and bake for 45-50 minutes, or until a toothpick inserted into the center of the cake comes out clean.
- If the top of the cake starts to brown too quickly, you can loosely cover it with aluminum foil halfway through baking.
- Once baked, remove the cake from the oven and let it cool in the pan for 10 minutes.
- Then, transfer the cake to a wire rack to cool completely.

6. Serve and Enjoy:

- Once the cake has cooled completely, slice it into thick slices.
- Serve and enjoy your delicious Vegan Marble Cake!
- Store any leftovers in an airtight container at room temperature for up to several days.

This Vegan Marble Cake is perfect for any occasion, from birthday parties to afternoon tea. The combination of vanilla and chocolate flavors swirled together makes it a delightful treat for vegans and non-vegans alike!

Vegan Chocolate Truffles

Ingredients:

- 1 cup vegan chocolate chips or chopped dark chocolate (at least 70% cocoa)
- 1/2 cup full-fat coconut milk (from a can)
- 1 teaspoon vanilla extract
- Pinch of salt
- Optional coatings: cocoa powder, shredded coconut, crushed nuts, powdered sugar, sprinkles, or melted vegan chocolate for dipping

Instructions:

1. Prepare the Chocolate Ganache:

- Place the chocolate chips or chopped chocolate in a heatproof bowl.
- In a small saucepan, heat the coconut milk over medium heat until it just begins to simmer.
- Pour the hot coconut milk over the chocolate and let it sit for a minute to soften the chocolate.
- Add the vanilla extract and a pinch of salt to the bowl.
- Stir the mixture with a whisk until the chocolate is completely melted and the mixture is smooth and glossy.

2. Chill the Mixture:

- Cover the bowl with plastic wrap or a lid and refrigerate the mixture for at least 2 hours, or until firm. The mixture should be scoopable but not too sticky.

3. Shape the Truffles:

- Once the mixture is chilled and firm, use a spoon or a small cookie scoop to portion out small balls of the chocolate ganache.
- Roll each portion between your palms to form smooth balls. Work quickly to prevent the mixture from melting too much.

4. Coat the Truffles:

- Roll the shaped truffles in your desired coatings, such as cocoa powder, shredded coconut, crushed nuts, powdered sugar, or sprinkles. Alternatively, you can dip them in melted vegan chocolate for an extra layer of chocolate.

5. Chill Again (Optional):

- Place the coated truffles on a baking sheet lined with parchment paper and refrigerate them for another 15-30 minutes to set the coatings.

6. Serve and Enjoy:

- Once the truffles are set, transfer them to an airtight container and store them in the refrigerator until ready to serve.
- Enjoy your delicious homemade Vegan Chocolate Truffles as a decadent treat or give them as gifts!

These Vegan Chocolate Truffles are rich, creamy, and perfect for satisfying your chocolate cravings. Feel free to customize them with different coatings or add-ins to suit your taste preferences.

Vegan Almond Joy Bars

Ingredients:

For the Coconut Layer:

- 2 cups shredded coconut (unsweetened)
- 1/2 cup coconut cream (from a can of full-fat coconut milk)
- 1/4 cup maple syrup
- 1 teaspoon vanilla extract
- Pinch of salt

For the Almond Layer:

- 1 cup raw almonds, whole or chopped
- 1/4 cup maple syrup
- 2 tablespoons coconut oil, melted
- 1 teaspoon almond extract
- Pinch of salt

For the Chocolate Coating:

- 1 cup vegan chocolate chips or chopped dark chocolate (at least 70% cocoa)
- 1 tablespoon coconut oil

Instructions:

1. Prepare the Coconut Layer:

- In a mixing bowl, combine the shredded coconut, coconut cream, maple syrup, vanilla extract, and a pinch of salt.
- Mix until well combined.

2. Press the Coconut Layer:

- Line an 8x8-inch square baking dish with parchment paper, leaving some overhang on the sides for easy removal.

- Press the coconut mixture evenly into the bottom of the prepared baking dish. Use a spatula or your hands to press it down firmly.

3. Prepare the Almond Layer:

    - In a food processor, pulse the raw almonds until they are finely chopped.
    - In a separate bowl, combine the chopped almonds, maple syrup, melted coconut oil, almond extract, and a pinch of salt. Mix until well combined.

4. Spread the Almond Layer:

    - Spread the almond mixture evenly over the coconut layer in the baking dish. Press it down gently with a spatula or your hands.

5. Chill the Bars:

    - Place the baking dish in the refrigerator and chill for at least 1 hour, or until the layers are firm.

6. Cut into Bars:

    - Once the bars are chilled and firm, use the parchment paper overhang to lift them out of the baking dish.
    - Transfer the bars to a cutting board and use a sharp knife to cut them into squares or bars.

7. Prepare the Chocolate Coating:

    - In a heatproof bowl set over a pot of simmering water (double boiler method), melt the vegan chocolate chips or chopped dark chocolate with the coconut oil. Stir until smooth and glossy.

8. Coat the Bars:

    - Dip each bar into the melted chocolate, coating it completely. You can also use a spoon to drizzle the chocolate over the bars.
    - Place the coated bars on a baking sheet lined with parchment paper.

9. Chill Again:

- Place the baking sheet in the refrigerator and chill the bars for another 15-30 minutes, or until the chocolate coating is set.

10. Serve and Enjoy:

- Once the chocolate coating is set, serve and enjoy your homemade Vegan Almond Joy Bars!
- Store any leftovers in an airtight container in the refrigerator for up to several days.

These Vegan Almond Joy Bars are a delicious and satisfying treat that's perfect for satisfying your sweet tooth. Enjoy the combination of coconut, almonds, and chocolate in every bite!

Vegan Cheesecake (Various flavors)

Ingredients:

For the Crust:

- 1 1/2 cups vegan graham cracker crumbs (or crushed vegan cookies)
- 1/4 cup coconut oil or vegan butter, melted
- 2 tablespoons maple syrup or agave syrup

For the Cheesecake Filling:

- 2 cups raw cashews, soaked in water for at least 4 hours or overnight, then drained
- 1/2 cup full-fat coconut milk (from a can)
- 1/2 cup maple syrup or agave syrup
- 1/4 cup coconut oil, melted
- 1/4 cup lemon juice
- 1 teaspoon vanilla extract
- Pinch of salt

For Flavor Variations:

Choose one of the following options to add flavor to your cheesecake:

For Classic Vegan Cheesecake:

- Omit additional flavorings.

For Chocolate Vegan Cheesecake:

- Add 1/4 cup cocoa powder to the filling mixture.

For Strawberry Vegan Cheesecake:

- Add 1 cup fresh or frozen strawberries to the filling mixture.

For Blueberry Vegan Cheesecake:

- Add 1 cup fresh or frozen blueberries to the filling mixture.

For Matcha Vegan Cheesecake:

- Add 1 tablespoon matcha powder to the filling mixture.

Instructions:

1. Prepare the Crust:

- Preheat your oven to 350°F (175°C). Grease a 9-inch springform pan.
- In a mixing bowl, combine the vegan graham cracker crumbs, melted coconut oil or vegan butter, and maple syrup or agave syrup. Mix until well combined.
- Press the mixture evenly into the bottom of the prepared springform pan.
- Bake the crust in the preheated oven for 10 minutes. Remove from the oven and let it cool while you prepare the filling.

2. Make the Cheesecake Filling:

- In a high-speed blender or food processor, combine the soaked and drained cashews, full-fat coconut milk, maple syrup or agave syrup, melted coconut oil, lemon juice, vanilla extract, and a pinch of salt.
- Blend on high until the mixture is smooth and creamy, scraping down the sides of the blender or food processor as needed.

3. Add Flavor (Optional):

- If making a flavored cheesecake, add the additional flavorings (cocoa powder, fruit, matcha powder, etc.) to the filling mixture and blend until well combined.

4. Assemble and Chill:

- Pour the cheesecake filling over the cooled crust in the springform pan, spreading it out evenly.
- Tap the pan gently on the countertop to remove any air bubbles.

- Place the cheesecake in the refrigerator to chill for at least 4 hours or until set.

5. Serve and Enjoy:

- Once the cheesecake is set, remove it from the springform pan and slice it into wedges.
- Serve your delicious Vegan Cheesecake with your desired toppings, such as fresh fruit, vegan whipped cream, or a drizzle of chocolate sauce.
- Enjoy your customized Vegan Cheesecake in various flavors!

Feel free to experiment with different flavor combinations and toppings to create your perfect vegan cheesecake. Store any leftovers in the refrigerator for up to several days.

Vegan Pistachio Baklava

Ingredients:

For the Pistachio Filling:

- 2 cups shelled pistachios, chopped
- 1/4 cup granulated sugar
- 1 teaspoon ground cinnamon

For the Syrup:

- 1 cup granulated sugar
- 1 cup water
- 1/2 cup maple syrup or agave syrup
- 1 tablespoon lemon juice
- 1 cinnamon stick (optional)
- Zest of 1 lemon (optional)

For the Baklava:

- 1 (16 oz) package vegan phyllo dough, thawed according to package instructions
- 3/4 cup vegan butter or melted coconut oil

Instructions:

1. Prepare the Pistachio Filling:

- In a mixing bowl, combine the chopped pistachios, granulated sugar, and ground cinnamon. Mix until well combined. Set aside.

2. Prepare the Syrup:

- In a saucepan, combine the granulated sugar, water, maple syrup or agave syrup, lemon juice, cinnamon stick (if using), and lemon zest (if using).
- Bring the mixture to a boil over medium heat, then reduce the heat to low and let it simmer for 10-15 minutes, stirring occasionally, until slightly thickened.

- Remove the saucepan from the heat and let the syrup cool to room temperature. Once cooled, remove the cinnamon stick and lemon zest (if using). Set aside.

3. Assemble the Baklava:

- Preheat your oven to 350°F (175°C). Grease a 9x13-inch baking dish.
- Unroll the thawed phyllo dough and place it between two damp kitchen towels to prevent it from drying out.
- Place one sheet of phyllo dough in the prepared baking dish and brush it lightly with melted vegan butter or coconut oil. Repeat with 7 more sheets of phyllo, brushing each sheet with butter or oil.
- Sprinkle a generous layer of the pistachio filling over the phyllo dough.
- Continue layering the phyllo dough and pistachio filling, using 8 sheets of phyllo in between each layer of filling. Finish with a layer of phyllo dough on top, brushing the top sheet with butter or oil.

4. Cut and Bake the Baklava:

- Use a sharp knife to cut the baklava into diamond or square shapes, being careful not to press down too hard and crush the layers.
- Bake in the preheated oven for 35-40 minutes, or until the baklava is golden brown and crispy.

5. Soak with Syrup:

- Remove the baklava from the oven and immediately pour the cooled syrup evenly over the hot baklava, allowing it to soak in.
- Let the baklava cool completely in the baking dish before serving.

6. Serve and Enjoy:

- Once cooled, serve your delicious Vegan Pistachio Baklava as a sweet treat or dessert.
- Store any leftovers in an airtight container at room temperature for up to several days.

Enjoy the rich flavors and crunchy layers of this veganized version of traditional pistachio baklava!

Vegan Tiramisu

Ingredients:

For the Cashew Cream:

- 2 cups raw cashews, soaked in water for at least 4 hours or overnight, then drained
- 1/2 cup full-fat coconut milk (from a can)
- 1/2 cup maple syrup or agave syrup
- 1/4 cup melted coconut oil
- 2 tablespoons freshly squeezed lemon juice
- 1 teaspoon vanilla extract
- Pinch of salt

For the Coffee Soaking Syrup:

- 1 cup strong brewed coffee, cooled
- 2 tablespoons maple syrup or agave syrup
- 2 tablespoons coffee liqueur (optional)

For Assembling the Tiramisu:

- 1 (7 oz) package vegan ladyfingers (savoiardi biscuits)
- Unsweetened cocoa powder, for dusting
- Vegan chocolate shavings, for garnish (optional)

Instructions:

1. Make the Cashew Cream:

- In a high-speed blender or food processor, combine the soaked and drained cashews, coconut milk, maple syrup or agave syrup, melted coconut oil, lemon juice, vanilla extract, and a pinch of salt.
- Blend on high until the mixture is smooth and creamy, scraping down the sides of the blender or food processor as needed.

2. Prepare the Coffee Soaking Syrup:

- In a shallow dish, whisk together the strong brewed coffee, maple syrup or agave syrup, and coffee liqueur (if using). Set aside.

3. Assemble the Tiramisu:

    - Quickly dip each vegan ladyfinger into the coffee soaking syrup, ensuring it's soaked but not soggy.
    - Arrange a layer of soaked ladyfingers in the bottom of a 9x9-inch square dish or individual serving glasses.
    - Spread half of the cashew cream over the layer of soaked ladyfingers, smoothing it out with a spatula.
    - Repeat with another layer of soaked ladyfingers and the remaining cashew cream.
    - Dust the top of the tiramisu with unsweetened cocoa powder using a fine mesh sieve.
    - Optionally, garnish with vegan chocolate shavings on top.

4. Chill and Serve:

    - Cover the tiramisu with plastic wrap and refrigerate for at least 4 hours, preferably overnight, to allow the flavors to meld and the tiramisu to set.

5. Serve and Enjoy:

    - Once chilled and set, slice the tiramisu into squares if using a dish, or serve directly from individual glasses.
    - Enjoy your delicious Vegan Tiramisu as a delightful dessert!

This vegan tiramisu captures the flavors and textures of the traditional Italian dessert while being dairy-free and cruelty-free. It's perfect for special occasions or anytime you're craving a decadent treat!

Vegan Lemon Bars

Ingredients:

For the Crust:

- 1 1/2 cups all-purpose flour
- 1/2 cup powdered sugar
- 1/2 cup vegan butter, softened
- Pinch of salt

For the Lemon Filling:

- 1 cup granulated sugar
- 1/4 cup cornstarch
- 1/2 cup freshly squeezed lemon juice
- Zest of 2 lemons
- 1 cup full-fat coconut milk (from a can)
- 1/4 cup water

Instructions:

**1. Preheat your oven to 350°F (175°C). Grease or line an 8x8-inch baking dish with parchment paper.

2. Make the Crust:

- In a mixing bowl, combine the all-purpose flour, powdered sugar, softened vegan butter, and a pinch of salt.
- Use a fork or pastry cutter to mix until the mixture resembles coarse crumbs and starts to come together.
- Press the mixture evenly into the bottom of the prepared baking dish.
- Bake the crust in the preheated oven for 15-18 minutes, or until lightly golden brown. Remove from the oven and set aside.

3. Prepare the Lemon Filling:

- In a saucepan, whisk together the granulated sugar and cornstarch until well combined.
- Stir in the freshly squeezed lemon juice, lemon zest, full-fat coconut milk, and water until smooth.
- Place the saucepan over medium heat and cook, stirring constantly, until the mixture thickens and comes to a gentle boil, about 5-7 minutes.
- Once the mixture has thickened, remove it from the heat and let it cool slightly.

4. Assemble and Bake:

- Pour the lemon filling over the baked crust, spreading it out evenly.
- Return the baking dish to the oven and bake for an additional 20-25 minutes, or until the filling is set.
- Remove from the oven and let the lemon bars cool completely in the baking dish.

5. Chill and Serve:

- Once cooled, place the lemon bars in the refrigerator to chill for at least 2 hours, or until firm.
- Once chilled, use a sharp knife to slice the lemon bars into squares.
- Dust the tops with powdered sugar before serving, if desired.
- Serve and enjoy your delicious Vegan Lemon Bars!

These vegan lemon bars are perfect for any occasion, from picnics to potlucks. They have a bright, tangy flavor and a buttery crust that will delight your taste buds!

Vegan Date Squares

Ingredients:

For the Date Filling:

- 2 cups pitted dates, chopped
- 1 cup water
- 1 tablespoon lemon juice
- Zest of 1 lemon (optional)
- 1/2 teaspoon vanilla extract

For the Oat Crust and Crumble:

- 2 cups old-fashioned rolled oats
- 1 cup all-purpose flour
- 1/2 cup brown sugar (or coconut sugar)
- 1/2 teaspoon baking soda
- 1/4 teaspoon salt
- 1/2 cup vegan butter or coconut oil, melted
- 1/4 cup maple syrup or agave syrup
- 1 teaspoon vanilla extract

Instructions:

**1. Preheat your oven to 350°F (175°C). Grease or line an 8x8-inch baking dish with parchment paper.

2. Make the Date Filling:

- In a saucepan, combine the chopped dates, water, lemon juice, and lemon zest (if using).
- Bring the mixture to a simmer over medium heat, stirring occasionally.
- Reduce the heat to low and continue to cook for about 10-15 minutes, or until the dates are soft and the mixture has thickened.
- Remove from heat and stir in the vanilla extract. Let the date filling cool slightly.

3. Prepare the Oat Crust and Crumble:

- In a large mixing bowl, combine the rolled oats, all-purpose flour, brown sugar, baking soda, and salt.
- Add the melted vegan butter or coconut oil, maple syrup or agave syrup, and vanilla extract to the dry ingredients.
- Stir until well combined and the mixture resembles a crumbly dough.

4. Assemble and Bake:

- Press half of the oat mixture evenly into the bottom of the prepared baking dish to form the crust.
- Spread the cooled date filling over the oat crust, smoothing it out with a spatula.
- Sprinkle the remaining oat mixture evenly over the date filling to form the crumble topping.

5. Bake the Date Squares:

- Bake in the preheated oven for 25-30 minutes, or until the top is golden brown.
- Remove from the oven and let the date squares cool completely in the baking dish.

6. Chill and Serve:

- Once cooled, transfer the date squares to the refrigerator to chill for at least 1 hour before slicing.
- Once chilled, use a sharp knife to slice the date squares into squares or bars.
- Serve and enjoy your delicious Vegan Date Squares!

These Vegan Date Squares are perfect for snacking, dessert, or even as a sweet breakfast treat. They're packed with fiber and natural sweetness from the dates, making them a healthier option for satisfying your sweet cravings!

Vegan Snickerdoodles

Ingredients:

For the Cookie Dough:

- 2 1/2 cups all-purpose flour
- 1 teaspoon baking soda
- 1/2 teaspoon cream of tartar
- 1/4 teaspoon salt
- 1 cup vegan butter, softened
- 1 1/4 cups granulated sugar
- 1/4 cup unsweetened applesauce
- 1 teaspoon vanilla extract

For the Cinnamon Sugar Coating:

- 1/4 cup granulated sugar
- 1 tablespoon ground cinnamon

Instructions:

**1. Preheat your oven to 350°F (175°C). Line a baking sheet with parchment paper.

2. Make the Cookie Dough:

- In a mixing bowl, whisk together the flour, baking soda, cream of tartar, and salt until well combined.
- In a separate large mixing bowl, cream together the softened vegan butter and granulated sugar until light and fluffy.
- Add the applesauce and vanilla extract to the creamed butter mixture, and beat until smooth and creamy.
- Gradually add the dry ingredients to the wet ingredients, mixing until a soft dough forms.

3. Prepare the Cinnamon Sugar Coating:

- In a shallow bowl or plate, mix together the granulated sugar and ground cinnamon until well combined.

4. Shape the Cookies:

- Scoop out tablespoon-sized portions of dough and roll them into balls using your hands.
- Roll each ball of dough in the cinnamon sugar mixture until evenly coated.

5. Bake the Cookies:

- Place the coated dough balls onto the prepared baking sheet, spacing them about 2 inches apart.
- Flatten each dough ball slightly with the bottom of a glass or the palm of your hand.
- Bake in the preheated oven for 10-12 minutes, or until the edges are set and the tops are slightly cracked.
- Remove from the oven and let the cookies cool on the baking sheet for 5 minutes before transferring them to a wire rack to cool completely.

6. Serve and Enjoy:

- Once cooled, serve your delicious Vegan Snickerdoodles with a glass of plant-based milk or your favorite hot beverage.
- Store any leftovers in an airtight container at room temperature for up to several days.

These Vegan Snickerdoodles are perfect for holiday baking, cookie swaps, or anytime you're craving a sweet and comforting treat. Enjoy the warm, cinnamon-spiced flavor in every bite!

Vegan Peanut Butter Cookies

Ingredients:

- 1 cup creamy peanut butter
- 1/2 cup granulated sugar
- 1/2 cup packed brown sugar
- 1/4 cup unsweetened applesauce
- 1 teaspoon vanilla extract
- 1 1/4 cups all-purpose flour
- 1/2 teaspoon baking soda
- 1/4 teaspoon salt

Instructions:

**1. Preheat your oven to 350°F (175°C). Line a baking sheet with parchment paper or lightly grease it.

**2. In a large mixing bowl, combine the creamy peanut butter, granulated sugar, brown sugar, applesauce, and vanilla extract. Mix until well combined and smooth.

**3. In a separate bowl, whisk together the all-purpose flour, baking soda, and salt.

**4. Gradually add the dry ingredients to the wet ingredients, stirring until a thick cookie dough forms.

**5. Using a tablespoon or a cookie scoop, scoop out portions of dough and roll them into balls. Place the dough balls onto the prepared baking sheet, leaving some space between each cookie.

**6. Use a fork to flatten each dough ball and create a crisscross pattern on top of each cookie.

**7. Bake the cookies in the preheated oven for 10-12 minutes, or until the edges are lightly golden brown.

**8. Remove the cookies from the oven and let them cool on the baking sheet for a few minutes before transferring them to a wire rack to cool completely.

9. Once cooled, serve and enjoy your delicious Vegan Peanut Butter Cookies!

These cookies are soft, chewy, and packed with peanut butter flavor. They're perfect for sharing with friends and family or enjoying as a sweet treat any time of day.

Vegan Chocolate Pudding Cake

Ingredients:

For the Chocolate Pudding Layer:

- 1 cup all-purpose flour
- 1/2 cup granulated sugar
- 1/4 cup cocoa powder
- 2 teaspoons baking powder
- 1/4 teaspoon salt
- 1/2 cup plant-based milk (such as almond or soy milk)
- 1/4 cup melted coconut oil or vegetable oil
- 1 teaspoon vanilla extract

For the Chocolate Cake Topping:

- 3/4 cup granulated sugar
- 1/4 cup cocoa powder
- 1 1/2 cups boiling water

Instructions:

**1. Preheat your oven to 350°F (175°C). Grease an 8x8-inch baking dish or cake pan.

2. Make the Chocolate Pudding Layer:

- In a mixing bowl, whisk together the all-purpose flour, granulated sugar, cocoa powder, baking powder, and salt until well combined.
- Add the plant-based milk, melted coconut oil or vegetable oil, and vanilla extract to the dry ingredients. Stir until a thick batter forms.
- Spread the batter evenly into the bottom of the prepared baking dish.

3. Make the Chocolate Cake Topping:

- In a separate mixing bowl, whisk together the granulated sugar and cocoa powder until well combined.
- Sprinkle the sugar-cocoa mixture evenly over the batter in the baking dish.

4. Pour the Boiling Water:

- Carefully pour the boiling water over the sugar-cocoa mixture in the baking dish. Do not stir.

5. Bake the Cake:

- Place the baking dish in the preheated oven and bake for 30-35 minutes, or until the cake is set and the top appears dry.
- The cake will rise to the top, and a thick chocolate pudding layer will form beneath.

6. Serve Warm:

- Once baked, remove the cake from the oven and let it cool slightly.
- Serve the Vegan Chocolate Pudding Cake warm, spooning the cake portion and pudding layer into bowls.

7. Optional Toppings:

- Serve with a dollop of vegan whipped cream or a scoop of dairy-free ice cream for an extra indulgent treat.

Enjoy the rich chocolate flavor and delightful contrast between the tender cake and creamy pudding layers in this Vegan Chocolate Pudding Cake!

Vegan Mint Chocolate Chip Cupcakes

Ingredients:

For the Cupcakes:

- 1 1/2 cups all-purpose flour
- 1 cup granulated sugar
- 1/4 cup cocoa powder
- 1 teaspoon baking soda
- 1/2 teaspoon salt
- 1 cup unsweetened almond milk (or any plant-based milk)
- 1/3 cup vegetable oil
- 1 tablespoon white vinegar
- 1 teaspoon vanilla extract
- 1/2 teaspoon mint extract
- 1/2 cup vegan chocolate chips

For the Mint Buttercream Frosting:

- 1/2 cup vegan butter, softened
- 2 cups powdered sugar
- 1-2 tablespoons unsweetened almond milk (or any plant-based milk)
- 1/2 teaspoon mint extract
- Green food coloring (optional)
- Vegan chocolate chips, for garnish (optional)

Instructions:

**1. Preheat your oven to 350°F (175°C). Line a muffin tin with cupcake liners.

2. Make the Cupcake Batter:

- In a large mixing bowl, whisk together the all-purpose flour, granulated sugar, cocoa powder, baking soda, and salt until well combined.
- In a separate bowl, mix together the almond milk, vegetable oil, white vinegar, vanilla extract, and mint extract.
- Pour the wet ingredients into the dry ingredients and mix until just combined.

- Fold in the vegan chocolate chips.

3. Fill the Cupcake Liners:

    - Spoon the cupcake batter into the prepared muffin tin, filling each cupcake liner about two-thirds full.

4. Bake the Cupcakes:

    - Place the muffin tin in the preheated oven and bake for 18-20 minutes, or until a toothpick inserted into the center of a cupcake comes out clean.
    - Once baked, remove the cupcakes from the oven and let them cool in the muffin tin for a few minutes before transferring them to a wire rack to cool completely.

5. Make the Mint Buttercream Frosting:

    - In a mixing bowl, beat the softened vegan butter until creamy.
    - Gradually add the powdered sugar, one cup at a time, beating well after each addition.
    - Add the almond milk, mint extract, and green food coloring (if using), and beat until smooth and fluffy. Adjust the consistency with more powdered sugar or almond milk if needed.

6. Frost the Cupcakes:

    - Once the cupcakes are completely cooled, frost them with the mint buttercream frosting using a piping bag or offset spatula.

7. Garnish (Optional):

    - Sprinkle the frosted cupcakes with vegan chocolate chips for garnish, if desired.

8. Serve and Enjoy:

    - Serve your Vegan Mint Chocolate Chip Cupcakes and enjoy the refreshing mint flavor combined with rich chocolate!

These Vegan Mint Chocolate Chip Cupcakes are perfect for any occasion, from birthday parties to St. Patrick's Day celebrations. They're sure to be a hit with vegans and non-vegans alike!

Vegan Coconut Cream Pie

Ingredients:

For the Pie Crust:

- 1 1/4 cups all-purpose flour
- 1/2 teaspoon salt
- 1/2 cup vegan butter, cold and cubed
- 3-4 tablespoons ice water

For the Coconut Cream Filling:

- 1 (14 oz) can full-fat coconut milk
- 1 cup unsweetened coconut milk beverage (from a carton)
- 1/2 cup granulated sugar
- 1/4 cup cornstarch
- 1/4 teaspoon salt
- 1 teaspoon vanilla extract
- 1 cup shredded coconut (unsweetened)
- Vegan whipped cream, for garnish (optional)
- Toasted coconut flakes, for garnish (optional)

Instructions:

1. Prepare the Pie Crust:

- In a large mixing bowl, whisk together the all-purpose flour and salt.
- Add the cold cubed vegan butter to the flour mixture and use a pastry cutter or fork to cut the butter into the flour until it resembles coarse crumbs.
- Gradually add the ice water, 1 tablespoon at a time, and mix until the dough starts to come together.
- Shape the dough into a disk, wrap it in plastic wrap, and refrigerate for at least 30 minutes.

2. Preheat your oven to 375°F (190°C).

3. Roll out the Pie Crust:

- On a lightly floured surface, roll out the chilled dough into a circle slightly larger than your pie dish.
- Carefully transfer the rolled-out dough to a 9-inch pie dish and trim any excess dough hanging over the edges. Crimp the edges of the pie crust as desired.

4. Blind Bake the Pie Crust:

- Line the pie crust with parchment paper or aluminum foil and fill it with pie weights or dried beans.
- Bake in the preheated oven for 15-20 minutes, or until the edges are lightly golden brown.
- Remove the parchment paper and weights, then return the crust to the oven and bake for an additional 5-7 minutes, or until the bottom is cooked through. Remove from the oven and let it cool completely.

5. Make the Coconut Cream Filling:

- In a medium saucepan, whisk together the full-fat coconut milk, unsweetened coconut milk beverage, granulated sugar, cornstarch, and salt until well combined.
- Place the saucepan over medium heat and bring the mixture to a gentle boil, stirring constantly.
- Once the mixture thickens and boils, remove it from the heat and stir in the vanilla extract and shredded coconut.

6. Assemble the Pie:

- Pour the coconut cream filling into the cooled pie crust, spreading it out evenly.
- Smooth the top with a spatula and place a piece of plastic wrap directly on the surface of the filling to prevent a skin from forming.
- Refrigerate the pie for at least 4 hours, or until the filling is set.

7. Serve and Garnish:

- Once the pie is chilled and set, remove it from the refrigerator.
- Optionally, garnish the pie with vegan whipped cream and toasted coconut flakes before serving.

8. Slice and Enjoy:

- Slice your Vegan Coconut Cream Pie and enjoy the creamy coconut filling and flaky crust!

This Vegan Coconut Cream Pie is a delicious dessert that's perfect for any occasion. It's creamy, coconutty, and completely dairy-free!

Vegan Raspberry Swirl Cheesecake

Ingredients:

For the Crust:

- 1 1/2 cups vegan graham cracker crumbs (or crushed vegan cookies)
- 1/4 cup coconut oil, melted
- 2 tablespoons maple syrup

For the Cheesecake Filling:

- 2 cups raw cashews, soaked in water for at least 4 hours or overnight, then drained
- 1/2 cup full-fat coconut milk (from a can)
- 1/2 cup maple syrup
- 1/4 cup lemon juice
- 1 teaspoon vanilla extract
- Pinch of salt

For the Raspberry Swirl:

- 1 cup fresh or frozen raspberries
- 2 tablespoons maple syrup
- 1 tablespoon lemon juice

Instructions:

1. Prepare the Crust:

- Preheat your oven to 350°F (175°C). Grease a 9-inch springform pan.
- In a mixing bowl, combine the vegan graham cracker crumbs, melted coconut oil, and maple syrup. Mix until well combined.
- Press the mixture evenly into the bottom of the prepared springform pan. Use the back of a spoon or a flat-bottomed glass to press it down firmly.
- Bake the crust in the preheated oven for 10 minutes. Remove from the oven and let it cool while you prepare the filling.

2. Make the Cheesecake Filling:

- In a high-speed blender or food processor, combine the soaked and drained cashews, full-fat coconut milk, maple syrup, lemon juice, vanilla extract, and a pinch of salt.
- Blend on high until the mixture is smooth and creamy, scraping down the sides of the blender or food processor as needed.

3. Prepare the Raspberry Swirl:

- In a small saucepan, combine the raspberries, maple syrup, and lemon juice.
- Cook over medium heat, stirring occasionally, until the raspberries break down and the mixture thickens slightly, about 5-7 minutes. Remove from heat and let it cool slightly.

4. Assemble the Cheesecake:

- Pour the cheesecake filling over the cooled crust in the springform pan, spreading it out evenly.
- Spoon dollops of the raspberry mixture on top of the cheesecake filling.
- Use a knife or toothpick to swirl the raspberry mixture into the cheesecake filling, creating a marbled pattern.

5. Chill and Serve:

- Place the cheesecake in the refrigerator and chill for at least 4 hours, or until set.
- Once chilled, remove the sides of the springform pan.
- Slice and serve your Vegan Raspberry Swirl Cheesecake.

6. Optional Garnish:

- Garnish slices of cheesecake with fresh raspberries and a dusting of powdered sugar, if desired.

Enjoy the creamy texture and tangy raspberry swirls of this Vegan Raspberry Swirl Cheesecake! It's a perfect dessert for any occasion.

Vegan Orange Cranberry Scones

Ingredients:

- 2 cups all-purpose flour
- 1/4 cup granulated sugar
- 1 tablespoon baking powder
- 1/2 teaspoon salt
- Zest of 1 orange
- 1/2 cup vegan butter or margarine, cold and cubed
- 1/2 cup dried cranberries
- 1/2 cup non-dairy milk (such as almond milk or soy milk)
- 1 tablespoon fresh orange juice
- 1 teaspoon vanilla extract
- 1 tablespoon maple syrup (for brushing)

Instructions:

**1. Preheat your oven to 400°F (200°C). Line a baking sheet with parchment paper.

**2. In a large mixing bowl, combine the all-purpose flour, granulated sugar, baking powder, salt, and orange zest. Mix until well combined.

**3. Add the cold, cubed vegan butter or margarine to the flour mixture. Use a pastry cutter or fork to cut the butter into the flour until the mixture resembles coarse crumbs.

**4. Stir in the dried cranberries until evenly distributed throughout the mixture.

**5. In a small bowl, mix together the non-dairy milk, fresh orange juice, and vanilla extract.

**6. Gradually pour the wet ingredients into the dry ingredients, stirring until a soft dough forms. Be careful not to overmix.

**7. Turn the dough out onto a lightly floured surface. Knead the dough gently a few times until it comes together.

**8. Pat the dough into a circle about 1 inch thick. Use a sharp knife to cut the circle into 8 wedges.

**9. Transfer the wedges to the prepared baking sheet, leaving some space between each scone.

**10. Brush the tops of the scones with maple syrup for a shiny finish.

**11. Bake in the preheated oven for 15-18 minutes, or until the scones are golden brown and cooked through.

**12. Remove from the oven and let the scones cool on the baking sheet for a few minutes before transferring them to a wire rack to cool completely.

**13. Serve and enjoy your Vegan Orange Cranberry Scones with a cup of tea or coffee!

These scones are best enjoyed fresh but can be stored in an airtight container at room temperature for up to 2 days. You can also freeze them for longer storage. Simply thaw at room temperature or gently reheat in the oven before serving.

Vegan Maple Pecan Pie

Ingredients:

For the Pie Crust:

- 1 1/4 cups all-purpose flour
- 1/4 teaspoon salt
- 1/2 cup vegan butter, cold and cubed
- 2-4 tablespoons ice water

For the Pecan Filling:

- 1 1/2 cups pecan halves
- 1 cup full-fat coconut milk (from a can)
- 3/4 cup maple syrup
- 1/4 cup brown sugar (or coconut sugar)
- 3 tablespoons cornstarch
- 1 teaspoon vanilla extract
- 1/4 teaspoon salt

Instructions:

1. Prepare the Pie Crust:

   - In a food processor, combine the all-purpose flour and salt. Add the cold, cubed vegan butter and pulse until the mixture resembles coarse crumbs.
   - Gradually add the ice water, 1 tablespoon at a time, pulsing until the dough starts to come together.
   - Transfer the dough to a lightly floured surface and shape it into a disk. Wrap in plastic wrap and refrigerate for at least 30 minutes.

2. Preheat your oven to 350°F (175°C).

3. Roll out the Pie Crust:

   - On a lightly floured surface, roll out the chilled dough into a circle large enough to fit your pie dish. Transfer the dough to the pie dish and trim any excess dough hanging over the edges. Crimp the edges as desired.

4. Prepare the Pecan Filling:

   - In a mixing bowl, combine the pecan halves, full-fat coconut milk, maple syrup, brown sugar, cornstarch, vanilla extract, and salt. Mix until well combined.

5. Assemble the Pie:

   - Pour the pecan filling into the prepared pie crust, spreading it out evenly.

6. Bake the Pie:

   - Place the pie in the preheated oven and bake for 45-50 minutes, or until the filling is set and the crust is golden brown. If the crust starts to brown too quickly, cover the edges with foil halfway through baking.
   - Remove the pie from the oven and let it cool completely before slicing.

7. Serve and Enjoy:

   - Once cooled, slice your Vegan Maple Pecan Pie and serve it with dairy-free whipped cream or ice cream, if desired.

Enjoy the rich, sweet flavors of this Vegan Maple Pecan Pie, a perfect dessert for any occasion!

Vegan Strawberry Rhubarb Crisp

Ingredients:

For the Filling:

- 3 cups sliced rhubarb (about 1/2-inch thick slices)
- 3 cups sliced strawberries
- 1/2 cup granulated sugar
- 2 tablespoons cornstarch
- 1 tablespoon lemon juice
- Zest of 1 lemon
- 1 teaspoon vanilla extract

For the Crisp Topping:

- 1 cup old-fashioned rolled oats
- 1/2 cup all-purpose flour
- 1/2 cup packed brown sugar
- 1/2 teaspoon ground cinnamon
- 1/4 teaspoon salt
- 1/2 cup vegan butter, cold and cubed

Instructions:

**1. Preheat your oven to 350°F (175°C). Grease a 9x9-inch baking dish or similar-sized oven-safe dish.

2. Make the Filling:

- In a large mixing bowl, combine the sliced rhubarb and strawberries.
- In a small bowl, mix together the granulated sugar and cornstarch. Add this mixture to the rhubarb and strawberries.
- Add the lemon juice, lemon zest, and vanilla extract to the bowl. Toss everything together until the fruit is evenly coated with the sugar mixture.

3. Prepare the Crisp Topping:

- In a separate mixing bowl, combine the rolled oats, all-purpose flour, brown sugar, ground cinnamon, and salt.
- Add the cold, cubed vegan butter to the bowl. Use your fingers or a pastry cutter to cut the butter into the dry ingredients until the mixture resembles coarse crumbs.

4. Assemble and Bake:

- Transfer the prepared fruit filling to the greased baking dish, spreading it out evenly.
- Sprinkle the crisp topping over the fruit, covering it completely.

5. Bake the Crisp:

- Place the baking dish in the preheated oven and bake for 40-45 minutes, or until the fruit is bubbly and the topping is golden brown.

6. Serve and Enjoy:

- Remove the crisp from the oven and let it cool slightly before serving.
- Serve your Vegan Strawberry Rhubarb Crisp warm, optionally with a scoop of dairy-free ice cream or whipped cream.

Enjoy the sweet-tart flavors of this Vegan Strawberry Rhubarb Crisp, a comforting and satisfying dessert that's perfect for any occasion!

Vegan Blueberry Lemon Bundt Cake

Ingredients:

For the Cake:

- 2 cups all-purpose flour
- 1 cup granulated sugar
- 1 teaspoon baking powder
- 1/2 teaspoon baking soda
- 1/4 teaspoon salt
- Zest of 2 lemons
- 1/3 cup fresh lemon juice
- 3/4 cup unsweetened almond milk (or any plant-based milk)
- 1/2 cup vegetable oil
- 1 teaspoon vanilla extract
- 1 1/2 cups fresh or frozen blueberries

For the Glaze:

- 1 cup powdered sugar
- 2-3 tablespoons fresh lemon juice
- Zest of 1 lemon (optional)

Instructions:

**1. Preheat your oven to 350°F (175°C). Grease and flour a bundt cake pan.

2. Make the Cake:

- In a large mixing bowl, whisk together the all-purpose flour, granulated sugar, baking powder, baking soda, salt, and lemon zest.
- In a separate bowl, combine the fresh lemon juice, unsweetened almond milk, vegetable oil, and vanilla extract.
- Pour the wet ingredients into the dry ingredients and mix until just combined.
- Gently fold in the blueberries until evenly distributed throughout the batter.

3. Bake the Cake:

- Pour the batter into the prepared bundt cake pan, spreading it out evenly.
- Bake in the preheated oven for 45-50 minutes, or until a toothpick inserted into the center comes out clean.
- Remove the cake from the oven and let it cool in the pan for 10 minutes before transferring it to a wire rack to cool completely.

4. Make the Glaze:

- In a small bowl, whisk together the powdered sugar and fresh lemon juice until smooth. Add more lemon juice as needed to achieve your desired consistency.
- Stir in the lemon zest, if using.

5. Glaze the Cake:

- Once the cake has cooled completely, drizzle the glaze over the top of the cake.
- Allow the glaze to set before slicing and serving.

6. Serve and Enjoy:

- Slice your Vegan Blueberry Lemon Bundt Cake and serve it with a cup of tea or coffee for a delightful treat!

Enjoy the bright flavors of lemon and juicy bursts of blueberries in this Vegan Blueberry Lemon Bundt Cake. It's sure to be a hit with vegans and non-vegans alike!

Vegan Chocolate Hazelnut Tart

Ingredients:

For the Crust:

- 1 1/2 cups finely ground hazelnuts
- 1 cup all-purpose flour
- 1/4 cup cocoa powder
- 1/4 cup granulated sugar
- 1/4 teaspoon salt
- 1/2 cup vegan butter, melted

For the Chocolate Hazelnut Filling:

- 1 cup hazelnuts, toasted and skins removed
- 1 cup full-fat coconut milk
- 1/2 cup vegan chocolate chips
- 1/4 cup cocoa powder
- 1/4 cup maple syrup
- 1 teaspoon vanilla extract
- Pinch of salt

For Garnish (Optional):

- Chopped hazelnuts
- Vegan chocolate shavings

Instructions:

1. Prepare the Crust:

- Preheat your oven to 350°F (175°C). Grease a 9-inch tart pan with a removable bottom.
- In a mixing bowl, combine the finely ground hazelnuts, all-purpose flour, cocoa powder, granulated sugar, and salt.
- Stir in the melted vegan butter until the mixture resembles coarse crumbs.

- Press the mixture evenly into the bottom and up the sides of the prepared tart pan.
- Bake the crust in the preheated oven for 10-12 minutes, or until set. Remove from the oven and let it cool slightly.

2. Make the Chocolate Hazelnut Filling:

- In a food processor or blender, blend the toasted hazelnuts until finely ground and resembling hazelnut butter.
- In a small saucepan, heat the coconut milk until it just begins to simmer.
- Place the vegan chocolate chips in a heatproof bowl. Pour the hot coconut milk over the chocolate chips and let it sit for a minute.
- Stir the chocolate mixture until smooth and well combined.
- Add the hazelnut butter, cocoa powder, maple syrup, vanilla extract, and a pinch of salt to the chocolate mixture. Stir until smooth and creamy.

3. Assemble the Tart:

- Pour the chocolate hazelnut filling into the cooled tart crust, spreading it out evenly.
- Smooth the top with a spatula.

4. Chill the Tart:

- Place the tart in the refrigerator to chill for at least 2 hours, or until the filling is set.

5. Garnish and Serve:

- Once chilled, garnish the tart with chopped hazelnuts and vegan chocolate shavings, if desired.
- Slice and serve your Vegan Chocolate Hazelnut Tart.

Enjoy the rich and decadent flavors of this Vegan Chocolate Hazelnut Tart! It's a perfect dessert for special occasions or anytime you're craving a delicious treat.

Vegan Mocha Brownies

Ingredients:

For the Brownies:

- 1 cup all-purpose flour
- 1/2 cup cocoa powder
- 1/2 cup granulated sugar
- 1/2 cup brown sugar
- 1/4 teaspoon salt
- 1/2 cup vegan butter, melted
- 1/4 cup brewed coffee, cooled
- 1/4 cup non-dairy milk (such as almond milk or soy milk)
- 2 tablespoons instant coffee granules
- 1 teaspoon vanilla extract

For the Mocha Glaze (Optional):

- 1/2 cup powdered sugar
- 1 tablespoon cocoa powder
- 1 tablespoon brewed coffee, cooled
- 1/2 teaspoon vanilla extract

Instructions:

**1. Preheat your oven to 350°F (175°C). Grease or line an 8x8-inch baking pan with parchment paper.

2. Make the Brownie Batter:

- In a large mixing bowl, whisk together the all-purpose flour, cocoa powder, granulated sugar, brown sugar, and salt until well combined.
- In a separate bowl, mix together the melted vegan butter, brewed coffee, non-dairy milk, instant coffee granules, and vanilla extract until the coffee granules are dissolved.
- Pour the wet ingredients into the dry ingredients and mix until just combined. Be careful not to overmix.

3. Bake the Brownies:

- Pour the brownie batter into the prepared baking pan, spreading it out evenly.
- Bake in the preheated oven for 25-30 minutes, or until a toothpick inserted into the center comes out with a few moist crumbs.
- Remove from the oven and let the brownies cool completely in the pan before slicing.

4. Make the Mocha Glaze (Optional):

- In a small bowl, whisk together the powdered sugar, cocoa powder, brewed coffee, and vanilla extract until smooth. Adjust the consistency by adding more coffee or powdered sugar as needed.

5. Glaze the Brownies (Optional):

- Once the brownies are cooled, drizzle the mocha glaze over the top using a spoon or piping bag.
- Allow the glaze to set before slicing and serving.

6. Serve and Enjoy:

- Slice your Vegan Mocha Brownies into squares and serve them with a cup of coffee or your favorite non-dairy milk.

These Vegan Mocha Brownies are rich, fudgy, and infused with the delicious flavor of coffee. They're perfect for satisfying your chocolate cravings with a hint of caffeine!

Vegan Cherry Chocolate Chip Muffins

Ingredients:

- 2 cups all-purpose flour
- 1/2 cup granulated sugar
- 1 tablespoon baking powder
- 1/2 teaspoon baking soda
- 1/4 teaspoon salt
- 1 cup non-dairy milk (such as almond milk or soy milk)
- 1/4 cup vegetable oil or melted coconut oil
- 1 teaspoon vanilla extract
- 1 cup fresh or frozen cherries, pitted and chopped
- 1/2 cup vegan chocolate chips

Instructions:

Preheat your oven to 375°F (190°C). Grease or line a muffin tin with paper liners.
In a large mixing bowl, whisk together the all-purpose flour, granulated sugar, baking powder, baking soda, and salt until well combined.
In a separate bowl, mix together the non-dairy milk, vegetable oil, and vanilla extract until well combined.
Pour the wet ingredients into the dry ingredients and stir until just combined. Be careful not to overmix.
Fold in the chopped cherries and vegan chocolate chips until evenly distributed throughout the batter.
Spoon the batter into the prepared muffin tin, filling each muffin cup about two-thirds full.
Bake in the preheated oven for 18-20 minutes, or until a toothpick inserted into the center of a muffin comes out clean.
Remove the muffins from the oven and let them cool in the muffin tin for a few minutes before transferring them to a wire rack to cool completely.
Once cooled, serve and enjoy your Vegan Cherry Chocolate Chip Muffins!

These muffins are perfect for breakfast, brunch, or as a snack on the go. The combination of sweet cherries and chocolate chips makes them irresistible!